Chinese dim sum cookbook for kids

Discovering culture, traditions, and tasty recipes of a Cantonese cuisine

Susanna Qin

© **Copyright 2023 - All rights reserved.**

The content contained within this book may not be reproduced, duplicated or transmitted without direct written permission from the author or the publisher.

Under no circumstances will any blame or legal responsibility be held against the publisher, or author, for any damages, reparation, or monetary loss due to the information contained within this book, either directly or indirectly.

Legal Notice:

This book is copyright protected. It is only for personal use. You cannot amend, distribute, sell, use, quote or paraphrase any part, or the content within this book, without the consent of the author or publisher.

Disclaimer Notice:

Please note the information contained within this document is for educational and entertainment purposes only. All effort has been executed to present accurate, up-to-date, reliable, and complete information. No warranties of any kind are declared or implied. Readers acknowledge that the author is not engaged in the rendering of legal, financial, medical or professional advice. The content within this book has been derived from various sources. Please consult a licensed professional before attempting any techniques outlined in this book.

By reading this document, the reader agrees that under no circumstances is the author responsible for any losses, direct or indirect, that are incurred as a result of the use of the information contained within this document, including, but not limited to, errors, omissions, or inaccuracies.

Contents

1. Introduction — 1
2. Traveling the World — 5
   Traditional Food
   A Trip Through Time and Places
3. All About Cantonese Food — 13
   What Is Cantonese Food?
   The Guangdong Region
   Characteristics of Cantonese Food
4. Tell Me About Dim Sum — 18
   The Dim Sum Experience
5. Sharing Is Caring — 25
   Why Are These Traditions Important?
   Family Time
6. Creating Dim Sum at Home — 30
   Tools
   Ingredients
7. Kitchen Safety — 35
   For Mom and Dad
   For You
8. Let's Cook! — 40

9. Recipes — 43
   - Steamed Pork Shaomai (or Shumai or Siuai)
   - Har Gow or Shrimp Dumplings
   - Char Siu Bao or Steamed Barbecue Pork Buns
   - Youtiao or Chinese Fried Dough Sticks
   - Zhaliang or Fried Dough Rice Noodle Rolls
   - Dim Sum-Style Gai Lan or Chinese Broccoli
   - Chinese Wu Tao Gou or Taro Cake
   - Easy-Peasy Steamed Ribs in Black Bean Sauce
   - Chicken Spring Rolls
   - Ngao Yuk or Cantonese Steamed Beef Balls
   - Cantonese Fried Noodles
   - Pork and Vegetable Rice Noodle Rolls
   - Congee or Chinese Rice Porridge
   - Yu Choy or Chinese Greens Stir-Fry
   - Chicken Pot Stickers or Dumplings
   - Chicken Dumpling Soup
   - Wonton Noodle Soup
   - Chicken Wonton Cups
   - Barbecued Chicken Dim Sum
   - Chive Pancakes
   - Chinese Sausage and Sticky Rice
   - Nai Wong Bao or Cantonese Steamed Custard Buns
   - Liu Sha Bao or Molten Custard Salted Egg Buns
   - Mango Pancakes
   - Egg Tarts

10. Teatime — 138
    - Bo Lay or Black Tea
    - Guk Fa or Chrysanthemum Tea
    - Guk Bo or Blended Black Tea and Chrysanthemum Tea

    Sau Mei Tea
    Luk Cha or Green Tea
    Red Tea

11. Conclusion   141

References   143

1
Introduction

How exciting is it to create a whole meal out of smaller items of food? I am always amazed at how you can throw together a bunch of different things and then end up with something completely new. It looks, smells, and tastes so different from the original ingredients—it is like being a wizard or magician and making magic!

I want you to have fun, get messy, ask lots of questions, experiment, and of course, make mistakes. As you go through this book, there will be times when you will need help, so do not be afraid to ask a grown-up. But of course, be brave, trust yourself, and be confident. There are no such things as silly questions—we are going to learn and have fun in the kitchen.

In this book, you and your parents will be making magical Cantonese food. You will be able to prepare, make, and serve your meals to your family and friends which is very rewarding. Being able to make things for your loved ones makes you and others feel good and appreciated.

Learning how to cook is a very important skill, and I am so glad to be on this adventure with you. Not only is it fun, but there are so many other skills that you can learn just by being in the kitchen. Gallagher (2019) has many reasons why you should be learning how to cook, and I agree with all of them.

Appreciation

Sometimes it can be easy to forget or see how much effort and love is put into cooking. Your mom and dad spend a lot of time preparing meals for you, and now, you will have the chance to see all the thought and work that goes into making sure your family is well-fed.

Remember to say "thank you" as it really is done with lots of love.

Different Tastes

Learning how to cook means you can experiment with different cuisines (such as dim sum) and ingredients. Cooking teaches you all about new foods and helps you get familiar with them.

I know that sometimes new things can be a bit scary at first, but cooking helps you overcome this and makes you more adventurous when it comes to food.

Confidence

Cooking shows you that you are capable in the kitchen. How cool is it to be able to serve a meal that you have cooked yourself? I think that is pretty awesome and it should be something that you are proud of. I want you to take pride and a sense of accomplishment in what cooking will provide and apply it to all the other areas of your life like sports.

Math

What does math have to do with cooking? Well, wait until you see a recipe. You will learn all about fractions and temperatures and even geometry. For example, measuring spoons are divided into different fractions of cups—half a cup, a quarter cup, or a third of a cup. Which one is bigger? Is a 9x9-inch pan the same as a 6x9?

Reading

Recipes will teach you a lot of new words that will improve your reading skills and vocabulary. Cooking also teaches you how to follow instructions and solve problems.

Science

What happens if you heat water to a certain point? What does yeast do and why? Cooking involves a lot of science and practical experiments that are great for learning about chemistry.

Health and Nutrition

Cooking and working with food will help you learn about health and nutrition. You will be able to explain which foods may be healthier than others and why. You will be creating fuel for your body—how amazing!

Origins of Food

There is quite a process that happens in order to get your meal to your table. The first thing you will do is get ingredients for your meal which can be found at the grocery store.

How did the ingredients get there?

Take dumpling wrappers, for example. They are made out of a lot of different ingredients like flour, water, oil, etc. Where do those ingredients come from? How do you make flour? These are all questions that might pop into your head while you are cooking, and it is the perfect time to ask and learn about where food comes from.

New Cultures

Different cuisines will introduce you to different cultures around the world. Dim sum is Cantonese cuisine, and you may or may not have known about it before reading this book. Spain has its own cuisine with its own special meals and cooking methods, and so do France and Africa. Every country has its own way of cooking and eating.

Cooking gives you a glimpse into the traditions of other cultures and helps you learn about all the various things that make us all unique and special. Our food culture is one of them.

Special Time Together

Spending time together in the kitchen is the perfect way to have fun, chat, and really pay attention to each other. This time is usually called bonding time, and all families should take some time to bond and do something fun that brings them closer.

So let's start having some fun.

2
Traveling the World

When it comes to exploring different cuisines, we must understand that food is more than just something we eat to fill our stomachs. Food is an essential part of culture, history, and tradition. Every culture has its unique dishes and ingredients, and learning about them is a fascinating journey that takes us to the heart of a country's traditions. We will fly together to China! Such a vast country with a rich culinary history!

China is big, the fourth biggest country in the world, and it has more than twenty regions. Each region has its unique cuisine that reflects its geography, climate, and cultural heritage. One of the most popular cuisines in China is Cantonese cuisine, which originated from the Guangdong province in the southern part of China. It is known for its delicate flavors, fresh ingredients, and the art of cooking that goes into preparing each dish.

Before we dive into the recipes of Cantonese cuisine, it is essential to understand the culture and traditions that have shaped this cuisine. By learning about the history and traditions behind a dish, we can gain a deeper understanding of its significance and meaning. For instance, many Cantonese dishes are associated with specific festivals, celebrations, or rituals. Understanding these associations can help us appreciate the cultural significance of the dish.

Moreover, understanding the culture and traditions behind a cuisine can give us insights into the ingredients and techniques used in preparing the dishes. In

Cantonese cuisine, for example, the use of fresh ingredients is a hallmark, as the people of Guangdong province are known for their love of seafood, vegetables, and fruits. The cuisine also places great emphasis on the art of cooking, with various techniques like stir-frying, steaming, and braising used to create distinct flavors and textures.

By exploring the culture and traditions behind Cantonese cuisine, we can gain a better appreciation of the unique flavors and ingredients that make it so special. It is a journey that will take us from the bustling streets of Guangzhou to the beautiful countryside of southern China, a journey that will deepen our understanding of the people, history, and traditions that have shaped this wonderful cuisine.

Traditional Food

Not only China but every country all over the world has its own unique traditions. You can think of a tradition as a special way of doing something. People have their traditional languages, religions, holidays, and even traditional clothes. That is what makes the world so wonderful. Everyone is different and interesting. Traditional food is one other thing that makes countries unique.

Food is an important part of Chinese culture. From business meetings to social gatherings with friends, eating has an important place in daily life and special occasions. Usually, there are many dishes that are served, and everyone takes part in sharing the meals with each other.

Cantonese food and culture originated from Guangdong, Hong Kong, and Macau in South China. In these regions, people primarily speak Cantonese, a dialect of Mandarin. Do you know that while the writing system remains the same, with the use of Chinese characters, the pronunciation of these characters is different between the two languages? For instance, the character for "China" is written as "　　" aǹd is pronounced as *ZhongGuo* in Mandarin, and as *ZhungGwok* in Cantonese.

Cantonese cuisine is one of the most well-known types of Chinese cuisine. From South Africa to America, Cantonese food can be found almost everywhere. I am pretty sure you have tried some Cantonese food. You may have ordered Cantonese takeout from your local restaurant or perhaps you visited Chinatown.

Chinatowns are areas where people whose families come from China live. They all come together as a big community of people so they can share their traditions. Remember we spoke about traditions earlier and how food is one of the unique things people share? In Chinatown, many of the restaurants will serve traditional Cantonese food. If you and your family have eaten at a restaurant here, the chances of you having eaten Cantonese food are very high.

Another spot you may have tried Cantonese food is at a dim sum restaurant. You may have gone there for brunch as people usually eat dim sum later on in the morning for either a late breakfast or early lunch which equals brunch.

Teahouses are also a part of Cantonese life and another place you may have visited where Cantonese food and drink were served. Teahouses are places to relax, socialize, and of course, drink tea.

So you see, there are many places within your city or suburb where you can find Cantonese food. All these traditional restaurants cropped up as the Chinese population grew within the country. So let's look at how and why they chose to settle in America.

A Trip Through Time and Places

Did you know that I am Chinese myself? So along with the research I did to get all the facts for you, I also have lots of past experiences, stories, and information that have been passed down to me from my family. Along with my personal knowledge, here are some of the things I found out from Britannica Kids (2020) about the history of the Chinese migration to America.

It is so interesting how things from one side of the world can be experienced all the way on the other side of the world. It is wonderful to think about how we can all be connected and learn from each other.

The original Chinese people were not born here; they were born in China and then moved here later on. This is known as immigration. Since then, many Chinese people have been born in this country, and their families have spent several years living here.

Chinese people first began to immigrate in the 1800s. Chinese workers arrived around 1820 to find work and build a life for themselves. Then a carpenter found some gold in California in 1949. Gold is a very valuable precious metal. This was the beginning of the gold rush which was when many people rushed to California hoping that they would find some gold as well (Britannica Kids, n.d.). This brought many more Chinese immigrants to America.

These immigrants also helped build the transcontinental railroad which is the railroad that linked the east of the United States to the west of the United States. The Chinese workers were an integral part of the construction, and many more relocated to America to work on the project.

Did you know there are over 10 million Asian Americans in the United States and that they have been a part of the culture for more than 150 years (Britannica Kids, n.d.)?

This is why there is such a bustling, thriving, and large Chinese population in certain areas of America. And by bringing over and continuing their traditions, we are lucky enough to experience their culture as well.

The Chinese also dispersed themselves to many other countries. One of the places they settled in was in Southeast Asia, specifically Singapore and Malaysia where they were traders and crafters. Australia and Western Europe were also popular places for them to settle, and you can find Chinatowns in various places here as well.

The Chinese worked hard and contributed greatly to the countries that they immigrated. They not only shared their talent for making delicious food but also helped grow the economy.

The biggest and most well-known Chinatowns can be found in the following places. As you will see, they are placed around the world in major cities (Sarah, 2016).

New York Chinatown

This is the largest Chinatown that can be found outside of China. The New York Chinatown was started by railroad workers around 1870. The workers chose to migrate from California to New York because people began to become anti-Asian.

This Chinatown is about 40 blocks big.

San Francisco

This hustling and bustling Chinatown takes the prize of the second biggest Chinatown outside of China. It is half the size of New York's Chinatown but just as vibrant and colorful.

Have you ever had a fortune cookie? The Golden Gate Fortune Cookie Factory can be found here. This is the company that makes these interesting little cookies that you find in Chinese restaurants around the world.

Vancouver

This Chinatown is the largest in Canada and the third largest in North America. It began in 1885.

This Chinatown not only provides traditional shopping experiences but is also known for the Dr. Sun Yat-Sen Classical Chinese Garden. This was built in the 1980s and is considered to be the first of its kind built outside of China. It was built in honor of Sun Yat-Sen who was the founder of modern China and is fondly referred to as the "Father of the Nation." Sun Yat-Sen did a number of influential things during his time as a leader, and to this day, he is considered one of the greatest Chinese leaders of his time.

Bangkok

Chinatown in Bangkok is one of the oldest in the world. It was created in 1767 when laborers and merchants relocated to try their luck and make their fortunes in the city.

Here, you can find a market that is 200 years old, many temples, and a solid gold Buddha that weighs five tons.

Toronto

Toronto has several Chinatowns, but the central Chinatown is the biggest and most popular among tourists. People moved to central Chinatown after the government demolished the original to make space to build a town hall.

London

The Chinatown that runs on either side of Gerrard Street, which lies between Leicester Square and Old Compton Street, was established in the 1950s when

Chinese migrants began to settle in the area. It hosts a grand Chinese New Year festival, which is well-known and celebrated yearly. It is well known for its vibrant food stalls, serving many different types of Chinese cuisine.

Manila

There are even Chinatowns all the way to the Philippines. The Chinatown in Manila has over one million inhabitants and was started in 1594. This makes it the oldest in the world. Like other Chinatowns, each street has a particular category of items that sells from office supplies to jewelry.

You can find a mix of influences here, including Italian, and along with other cultural elements, there are both old traditional stores and businesses mixed in with more modern newer businesses.

Singapore

Raffles Hotel is a long-standing chain of hotels that was established in Singapore and helped with the planning of the town. When planning the town, Raffles decided to assign certain areas to certain races, thus creating a Chinatown within Singapore.

Now the smaller traditional stores of Chinatown sit among the modern skyscrapers.

Paris

The Chinatown in Paris can be found between Avenue d'Italie and Avenue d'Ivry. Here, there are abundant tearooms and noodle bars as well as gift and clothing shops.

Melbourne

Chinatown was established in Melbourne in 1850 when thousands of Chinese migrated to Australia hoping to find their fortunes mining gold just like their countrymen did during the California Gold Rush.

The Chinese Museum is located in Chinatown and is a great place to learn about the history of the Chinese in Australia.

The impact of Chinese culture is found in so many different countries from France to Canada and even the Philippines, so we must remember that each dish in each country will be slightly different as it takes on influences of the local area. Now you will be able to experience Cantonese cuisine in your home and add your unique twist to your meals.

3
All About Cantonese Food

Before we get to the kitchen, I want to give you more information about the food you will be cooking. I mentioned some interesting facts at the beginning of the book, but now is the time for you to learn more about the history and culture of Cantonese food.

I believe it is very important because it will not only help you understand the culture of the food but also appreciate all the elements involved in how and why it is made the way it is.

What Is Cantonese Food?

You may be wondering what the difference is between Chinese food and Cantonese food. Cantonese food is also known as Yue cuisine, and it is a food that comes from a particular region in China.

Remember that different countries have different traditions and ways of doing things, of which cooking is one. Well, some countries can be so big that within these areas are smaller regions that have their own traditions as well. China is just like that. There are several smaller areas within China that have created their own practices and ways of doing things that differ from others. Cantonese-style cooking is one of these differences.

So we can say that Cantonese food is Chinese food but just one of the different food traditions of the country.

Cantonese food is the most well-known type of food outside of China, so when most people think of Chinese food, they may be thinking of Cantonese food in particular. Cantonese is also the most widely spoken dialect in American Chinatowns.

The Guangdong Region

The Guangdong Region, which is where Cantonese food originates, has six major cities which are Dongguan, Foshan, Guangzhou, Shantou, Shenzhen, and Zhongshan. It is also very close to Hong Kong and Macau which is why it has had such an influence on those cities' traditional food (Eye on Asia, n.d.).

I am from Guangzhou which is the capital of Guangdong. I want to share some interesting facts with you about my hometown.

About 14 million people live in this capital city. Guangzhou was also awarded the prestigious honor of being the capital city of China three times. The city is based along a coastline and is a trading port. In fact, it is one of China's most important ports

As a port city, it has had a lot of exposure and access to different ingredients such as meat and vegetables which have played a role in influencing the cuisine.

Characteristics of Cantonese Food

Whereas a lot of the different regions rely heavily on spices and herbs to add flavor to their dishes, Cantonese food likes to keep things simple. Cantonese recipes call for fresh ingredients, and these are a must for creating the dishes that many love and enjoy eating.

Dishes make use of lovely fresh vegetables, delicious succulent cuts of meat, and interesting sweet sauces. They are not usually spicy in nature, focusing more on highlighting the natural flavors of the main ingredients. That's not to say that they do not use spices at all; they most certainly do. The popular ones are pepper, chili, ginger, and garlic. They also pick their herbs and spices depending on the season, meaning they stick to locally grown food that is available at that time of year.

There are many different ways to cook food, steaming, boiling, grilling, and frying—I could go on and on listing the various ways food is prepared, but there are certain tried and tested ways that Cantonese food is made. Food is prepared very simply and with great care and is usually steamed, poached, or simmered. These particular methods of cooking help to highlight every single ingredient's special flavor.

Although these are the favorite methods of cooking, chefs do use other ways to prepare the food depending on the dishes they are serving. These include stir-frying, boiling, baking, braising, roasting, or sauteing. You will be using some of these methods when you begin to experiment in the kitchen a little later on.

You will also notice that there are certain elements to Cantonese food, and you will find the following elements on some of your local restaurant's menus:

- fresh and dried seafood

- soups

- sauces like hoisin, oyster, and plum

- dried or barbequed meats such as duck and pork

Cantonese food is considered to be quite healthy, which is why I love cooking it and serving it to my family.

Sugar isn't the healthiest of foods, and Cantonese food uses a lot less sugar than a lot of other cuisines. This makes it better for your health. Plus Cantonese food contains a lot of vegetables. In fact, vegetables are often the most important part of the meal. Sometimes most meals see vegetables as just side dishes, but Cantonese food makes them the hero.

You have probably heard about carbohydrates, which are food that our body uses to create energy to help us do all the activities we do every day. There are carbohydrates that are very good for you and carbohydrates that are not so great, and we should try to eat less of them. These are called refined carbohydrates, which means that all the good stuff like nutrients, vitamins, and minerals have been removed from them. Cantonese foods are very low in refined carbohydrates and contain lots of good carbs. To stay healthy, we want to make sure that most of our meals are just like that—full of good carbs.

There are a lot of popular Cantonese dishes. Do you have a favorite? Perhaps it is one from this list:

- spring rolls
- Cantonese steamed chicken
- Cantonese beef curry
- sweet and sour pork
- ginger–soy steamed fish
- red bean soup

These are just a couple of the most popular dishes that can be found at your closest Cantonese restaurant or in a cookbook like this one. But before we get to the cooking part, we are going to look at one of the most well-known Cantonese dishes: dim sum.

4
Tell Me About Dim Sum

Dim sum is a meal, usually eaten around brunch time, that consists of small plates of snacks and dumplings. It is usually accompanied by tea; this is called yum cha.

Here is some history behind the meal from Asia Society (n.d.). According to them, the idea of dim sum began once the teahouses in the port city of Guangzhou became popular. This was in the late 19th century. Travelers would often stop at teahouses to rest, drink tea, and eat dim sum. This tradition caught on and spread around the region and then to other countries when the migrant workers headed west.

You can find dim sum or yum cha easily in any Chinatown or city across the world. These places usually include dishes, ingredients, and traditions from other Chinese and Western cuisines making each dining experience unique in some way.

The Dim Sum Experience

The small plates of dim sum are meant to be shared among the eaters. In fact, dim sum means "touch the heart" which means that these small meals were eaten to just satisfy your hunger and not fill you up completely (Yauatcha, 2019).

Dim sum is usually a midmorning meal, but there are some restaurants in Hong Kong that open up as early as 5 a.m. The sun may not have even risen by then, but the tea will be ready to serve. And since they open so early in the morning, they also usually close earlier in the day.

This may not be the case for some of your local yum cha restaurants as they may have adopted the Western practice of eating dim sum for dinner as well.

Regardless of when you decide to go to your local restaurant or teahouse, there are some rules when ordering dim sum. The first thing you and your parents should do is pick a tea that you want to drink. Once you have picked your tea, the person closest to the teapot should be in charge of pouring the tea for the guests before they pour themselves a cup.

Once you have enjoyed your tea and would like some more, take off the teapot lid and rest it either on top of the teapot or to the side. This is like a super secret signal to your waiter to refill the teapot.

Now for ordering your dim sum. Most restaurants you have been to would have provided you with menus when you sat down at your table, but in traditional dim sum restaurants, this is a little different. Instead of a menu, visitors will choose their dim sum from a cart that is pushed through the restaurant by a waiter. As he stops at your table or your parents call him over, you can take a look at all the different dim sum he has and select the plates you want to eat. Don't worry, he will keep track by marking a card with your order. Another way that this is done is that you will be given a "menu card" of your own, and you keep track of the plates you have ordered.

Tables are usually round and have a big glass plate in the middle that can rotate; this is where the waiter will place your dim sum. This round rotating centerpiece helps each person reach their favorite dim sum. In order to keep it warm, it will be served in a steamer basket.

The waiter should provide you with a small dish, chopsticks, a spoon, a bowl, and a teacup for your meal.

There is a certain way and order that each type of food comes out—it follows a plan. The first plates to be served are usually steamed dishes. These dishes are usually lighter on your stomach and do not fill you up too much. It saves room for the deep-fried dishes that come afterward. And don't worry, the last and the best dish which is the dessert comes out last.

If you think about it, this makes a lot of sense—you don't fill yourself up too early on in the meal and will still have room for all the delicious small servings of dim sum you want to have. It is kind of similar to having small starters, a main, and a dessert.

Along with the rules about when and in what order you should eat your dim sum, there are also some guidelines as to how you should eat it. You want to make the most of your experience and make sure you get to taste all the delicious ingredients and love that has been put into creating dim sum. Here are some things to remember while you munch away at your meal (Millson, 2017).

Take Small Bites

Think like a mouse and nibble; do not chomp like a hungry hippo. The best way to really get all the delicious flavor is to eat each dim sum in small bites, unlike sushi which you just pop into your mouth.

Another reason to eat slowly and carefully is that some dishes are made with soup which can be very hot. You could burn your mouth if you are not too careful.

Save the Soy

As you will learn as you begin cooking, a good chef will season their food before serving. Try out your dim sum before adding any soy to it as this may make it too salty and hide the flavor of all the delicious ingredients.

But of course, at the end of the day, listen to your taste buds and do what makes them happy!

Use Your Spoon

Your spoon can be used to sip the broth and the soup, but you can also use it to help you eat the other food on your plate. Your spoon can help you remove meat from the bone and help keep your food still while you try to eat it.

Do Not Share Chopsticks

Be mindful when you are using chopsticks, and do not use your set to touch another person's food. Your chopsticks have been in your mouth, and you rather not share your saliva with others, right? There are certain utensils for eating and certain utensils for serving, and they need to be separate.

Your waiter should provide you with a pair of chopsticks that you can use to serve the meals. These extra pairs of chopsticks will ensure that nobody uses their own to touch other's food. If this pair is missing, ask your waiter for it.

If you cannot use chopsticks, it is perfectly fine to ask for and use a fork.

I know how fun it is to play with chopsticks and pretend they make drumsticks or monster fangs, but please do not play with them.

There Are Secret Codes

Remember that the signal for more tea is to place the teapot lid on top or to the side of the teapot. Well, there are other hand signals that are used to communicate as well. If you want to say thank you, tap your index finger and middle finger together on the table.

Go Back for Seconds and Thirds

I know this food is so delicious and you may not know what you want, so you are tempted to order as much as you can. Remember, you can also go back and order more. Start off with a couple of small plates and go from there. You do not want any leftovers to go to waste, and you shouldn't get them in a doggy bag as they do not taste as good the next day.

Some of the most popular dim sum dishes you can order are dumplings (steamed but also fried), buns, meat plates, green vegetables, sweets, and little cakes. Here is a breakdown of the different kinds of dim sum.

Steamed

- dumplings, bao, shumai, and jiaozi
- braised meats and spareribs
- steamed seafood
- steamed rolls with different fillings

Soups

- bird's nest soup, congee, and abalone
- poached fish, seafood, and chicken in broth

Rice

- fried rice wrapped in lotus leaves
- zongzi, also known as rice dumplings, which have various fillings
- rice casseroles with steamed chicken

Buns

- pineapple buns, custard buns, and honey-glazed buns

Fried

- spring rolls, turnips, and taro cakes
- scallion pancakes
- panfried dumplings
- battered deep-fried meat and seafood
- deep-fried rice balls with fillings
- chicken feet

Desserts

- egg tarts and mango pudding
- thousand-layer cake and sponge cake
- bean curd puddings and red bean soups
- rice in coconut cream

As you can see, there is a wide variety of dishes so everyone is sure to find their favorite.

Did you see that we mentioned chicken feet? Cantonese food makes use of all the edible parts of meat—this is great because it means that nothing really goes to waste.

We call this sustainable eating, and it is so good for our environment to be more aware of what we eat and not waste food. Often these parts of meat are filled with lots of vitamins and minerals and are high in protein and iron. So although at first, it may seem weird to eat chicken feet, remember that every country has its own unique food traditions, and what seems weird to us is not to others.

Have fun discovering all these new and interesting flavors as well as the different customs of Cantonese culture.

5
Sharing Is Caring

We have a saying in our house that goes, "Sharing is caring." And eating dim sum is all about sharing with your family and friends. Food not only fuels your body, but it also brings people together.

Think about dinnertime and how fun it is to chat about your day and share stories with your family. Or think about lunchtime at school, eating your lunch with your friends and sharing your favorite toys, or the joy you get when you are sharing an ice cream at the beach with your brother or sister.

Sharing and eating as a community are something that humans have been doing for years and years.

Do you know we are actually known as "social animals" which means that we like, want, and need to be around other people to be happy and to thrive?

If we look back on history, we will see that at one stage we all lived together as hunter-gatherers. The men would usually go out and hunt for food while the women would go looking for and collecting it. The food would then be shared and eaten with the rest of the group.

Food and eating form a part of our celebrations. People often have special restaurants that they go to when they want to celebrate important occasions. We host dinner parties or lunches and invite our friends and family to spend time with us and eat. We make special cakes to celebrate our birthdays or weddings.

As you can see, food is a very important aspect of our lives.

Just like dim sum, many other cultures have their own traditional foods that are shared.

The Spanish have tapas, North Africa and the Middle East have meze, Italy has apericena, and Mexico has antojitos. In India, people share samoosas and spiced nuts and seeds along with other baked goods, and the Greeks love to share bowls of olives, feta, and dried fish.

Sharing, and sharing your food, helps bring us all closer and feel connected to each other which is very important as human beings.

Why Are These Traditions Important?

Traditions within a culture are important in maintaining identity and history. Traditions are passed down from parent to children, who will then pass them on to their children, and so the cycle continues and our knowledge is shared and kept alive.

The Chinese have a long tradition of sharing meals that began hundreds of years ago. There is important symbolism involved in eating together. Symbolism means that an object can stand in place for something else, like a country's flag stands in place for the country (Kids Connect, 2017).

In Chinese tradition, eating together around round tables, with round plates and bowls, symbolizes unity and togetherness (Keats, n.d.). Families will wait for everyone to be home before starting a meal, and coworkers will invite one another to lunch. This is all done with the goal to build "Guan Hei" which means relationship (Joyful House Team, 2021). Relationships are built around the table as family and friends chat about what to order or which was the most delicious.

It is the time of the day when everyone can relax and have fun.

After a busy day, where everyone may be out and about, getting together for a meal is a way to reconnect with your family. Going out to a dim sum restaurant or hosting a dim sum dinner party is the perfect way to gather your family and friends together. The more the merrier!

Mealtime Traditions

In Chinese culture, there are many traditions that are observed during mealtimes, both at restaurants and during meals at home.

It is best to start your meal with the plates of food that are closest to you. You can use your chopsticks to fill your plate with what you would like to eat before you pass it to the person sitting next to you. Even if you see a special piece of food that you want to eat, do not spend time digging around for it as this is considered rude.

Here's a little trick that I love. If you want to show extra special love and affection to someone at the table, then give them a very delicious serving of food. This is a sign of affection and lets them know you are thinking fondly of them.

Everyone is important and has their own special place within a family. This is called hierarchy. Mealtimes are a good way to show respect to everyone who fits in a family's hierarchy.

If you have a special guest visiting, they will normally be seated facing the entrance to the dining area, then the second and third special guests will be seated to their left and right, and along we go as all the special people at our table get their own special spot to sit.

It may end up that you or your younger sibling or cousin or friend will be seated right opposite the oldest member of the group. How fun!

As a sign of respect, the most delicious food is placed in front of the head of the family or special guests, and it is the youngest person in the group who will invite them to begin eating. They will then pick up their chopsticks and begin to eat their meal which is a signal to everyone else to begin.

When you are done, place your chopsticks next to your plate. Remember that it is considered rude to leave your chopsticks in your bowl or stuck in unfinished food.

Family Time

We spoke about the symbolism of unity that eating together represents earlier, and I want to touch on how important family time is.

Dim sum is a special occasion for families to spend time together and appreciate each other. Often life is very busy with parents going off to work and children off to school. Families can also live far away from each other and only come together on certain special occasions. Dim sum can bring us closer.

Chinese culture places a lot of importance on family, and often many generations of family will live in one house—grandparents, parents, and children. If families do not live together, they will then make an effort to see each other often and spend time together over holidays as well.

A dim sum shared with family is important. Our time together with our loved ones and friends is special, and we should be grateful that we have the opportunity to share food with each other. Grandparents, cousins, aunts, uncles, and friends play important roles in our lives, and we should appreciate the different things they can teach us.

Sometimes it is easy to get distracted and absorbed in video games, cell phones, and television, so it's essential to try and stay present when we get these moments with our families.

Speaking of distractions, dim sum restaurants can be very noisy as they are social places where people come together to chat and enjoy each other's company. Often this can be pretty overwhelming. There is always something going on, either food being delivered, tea being poured, or general conversation and laughter. This friendly chaos adds to the joy of being there. The opportunity to talk to each other and share is a wonderful aspect of this kind of dining experience. It teaches us to listen carefully and interact politely with one another.

Dim sum gives us the perfect environment to practice our social skills and be the social beings that we are. This creates happiness, closeness, and strong bonds between us.

6
Creating Dim Sum at Home

Chefs, we are about to get to the fun and practical part of the book! We are going to gather the tools we will need to create our own dim sum in our kitchen.

Tools

Steamers

Traditional steamers are made out of bamboo, but a stainless steel one will also work. You want to try to get a wide steamer that fits across a wide pot—the more space the better as there needs to be enough space in between the dumplings for them to cook properly.

Dumpling steamer liners

We do not want our food sticking to the steamer, and these dumpling steamer liners will make sure that that does not happen.

Wok

A wok is a bowl-like frying pan and is a must for any Chinese cooking. Woks allow oil to stay hot at the bottom of the pan, and you can use a spatula to move the food through it. This means you do not need to use a lot of oil to cook which makes food a lot healthier and makes it easier to make your dumplings crispy. Yum!

Pots and pans

You may need additional pots and pans to cook other ingredients such as rice as well as to deep-fry certain dishes. You will also need a pot that is the same size as your steamer to use to steam your food in.

Wire sieve, bamboo strainer, and fine wire mesh strainer

A wire sieve or bamboo strainer is used to deep-fry food. The sieves make sure that you do not spill oil as you add and remove food as well as ensure that your dumpling fillings do not spill out into the pot. If the filling does fall out, a fine wire mesh strainer will remove these bits.

It can also be used to strain your soups and broths.

Metal spatula and ladle

A spatula and ladle are cooking utensils that will help you cook and prepare your dim sum. The ladle is used to add the food to the wok, while the spatula can be used to fill the dumplings and move the food around the wok as it cooks.

Chopsticks

Do I really need to say more about why we need chopsticks? To eat our food of course! This is the ultimate utensil and a must for all Asian meals. According to Asian Inspirations (2019), chopsticks are believed to have been created in China about 3,000 years ago.

Chopsticks are the perfect tool because they force you to take smaller portions of your food and savor each bite.

Did you know that the round tip at the bottom of the chopsticks symbolizes earth and the square at the top of the chopsticks symbolizes heaven?

Porcelain soup spoon

A porcelain soup spoon is used for eating soup as well as for eating soup dumplings. They are usually made from porcelain as it is able to withstand heat better so you are less likely to burn your tongue and mouth. These spoons do not look like your traditional spoons as they have a larger scoop and a shorter handle.

Bowls

These are used for serving rice, soup, or broth. The size of the bowls is perfect for you to have a small serving and then go back for more if you want. These bowls are also usually made of porcelain as they retain the heat very well and help keep the food warm.

A teapot and cups

A tea set usually comes with a brewing pot, brewing tray, tea pitcher, and cups.

You can find all the tools you need to create dim sum from your local Asian store in Chinatown or online. There are many online stores that stock all you need including specialty ingredients and will deliver them to your home.

Ingredients

The ingredients you will need depend on the recipes you will be making, but there are a couple of important things that you can have on hand that you will make use of regardless of what you may be making.

Firstly, you need to ensure that all your ingredients are fresh. This is very important when making dim sum as the natural flavors are one of the main characteristics of good dim sum.

Wrappers

Keep some spring rolls, dumplings, and wonton wrappers in your freezer.

Various flour

Rice flour, tapioca starch, potato starch, and wheat starch are all flours that are used when preparing dim sum, particularly rice rolls.

Soy sauce

Soy sauce is a very well-known condiment, and it is used in many dishes. You get regular and dark soy sauce, and I suggest you have both available in your kitchen.

There are many different brands, so you may have one that is your favorite. Did you know that different countries have soy sauces that can differ in taste, color, and saltiness?

Sesame oil

Sesame oil helps give Asian food its particular, very recognizable Asian flavor. It is usually used in stir-fries.

Oyster sauce

This sauce is a must-have ingredient for anyone looking to cook Cantonese cuisine.

Garlic

Garlic forms the foundation for many recipes, and you should always have some cloves on hand.

Ginger

Ginger is a very recognizable and distinct flavor that goes well with seafood dishes.

Spring onions

Also known as scallions, this is another pantry must-have. They are used in stir-fries and other various Cantonese dishes.

Bean curd sheets

Bean curd is made from soy. You make bean curd by boiling soy milk and carefully lifting off the skin which forms on top. They can be sold fresh, frozen, or dried.

Cooking methods

There are various ways to cook food, and before we get to the recipes, I want to tell you what these methods are.

Steaming

Steaming is the process of cooking food by using hot steam. You can steam vegetables, meat, buns, bread, dumplings, and desserts.

Steaming food is one of the healthiest ways to cook food as you do not need any oil. Most dim sum dishes are cooked using this method.

Deep-frying

Deep-frying creates crispy food. Dim sums such as sesame prawn toast and pot stickers are usually fried.

Baking

You bake food in an oven. The oven produces dry hot heat that cooks the food. The air moves around the oven and can be heated up to 300 °F. Custard tarts and pork roast buns are usually cooked in an oven.

7
Kitchen Safety

The kitchen is a wonderful and magical place. It is a place where we can get messy, experiment, and create. Like scientists and witches and wizards, we take the ordinary and turn it into something extraordinary.

As much fun as it is to be in the kitchen making delicious food, we also need to remember that there are a lot of things that we need to be mindful of. I have some rules for both you and your parents to follow so we can have lots of fun and be safe as well.

For Mom and Dad

Hi, mom and dad or aunty and uncle. Here are some things to consider when you and your child are in the kitchen together so that you both can be safe and have a great time together.

Patience

It may take a little longer and it may be a lot messier but it is all worth it, I promise. You are teaching them invaluable lessons and creating special memories. Breathe and embrace the time together. Here are some tips to make the process a bit less stressful for you, courtesy of Lindsay Livingston (2020) of the Lean Green Bean.

Set up an easily accessible bin

All food waste can be easily disposed of here and saves you numerous trips back and forth to the bin. It may also help to set up some spoon holders to keep the counters slightly cleaner and the utensils in order.

Limit the workspace

Pick a specific area that you will work in and try to keep to that space. You can even set up an old sheet or piece of plastic on the floor around that area to catch any spills that may occur. Be sure to pick age-appropriate tasks for them. For example, older kids may be comfortable cutting up ingredients while the younger ones can be in charge of measuring or mixing.

Let them help you clean up

Cleaning up is an important lesson to learn about cooking. Better yet, teach them to keep things tidy as they go along. Put ingredients away after you have used them, wipe surfaces as you go, and, load the dishwasher with dishes you have already used.

Remember to be reasonable—there are going to be mistakes, misread-over, and maybe some tears, but it is all a part of the learning process for you and them.

Give them a tour of the kitchen

Take some time to explain where everything is kept and why. Show them the appliances and utensils they will be using and how they work. Make sure that you are clear about what they should be careful around and why. Take this time to explain the rules clearly, and make sure they feel comfortable in the kitchen which will also make them more confident.

Be mindful of your environment

We have spent many years in the kitchen, and it is easy to resort to autopilot when we do certain things. It may seem like common knowledge, but this may be an unfamiliar place for your kids.

Keep the handles of the pots turned away from the front of the stove; this minimizes the chance of it being accidentally knocked over. Be mindful of the hot stove, oven, and pots. Food that is freshly cooked will also be warm so be sure to wait before tasting it. Finally, remember to turn off and unplug any appliances you are finished using.

For You

Here are some kitchen rules for you to follow. These rules will make sure you are having lots of fun while being safe at the same time. They are very easy to follow and don't worry, your assistant chefs will be there to guide you.

Ask for permission

Always ask for permission before cooking. If this is your first time in the kitchen, your mom, dad, or the adult you are working with will give you a kitchen tour to make sure you are comfortable in the space. They will let you know how to work certain appliances, where different pots and pans or utensils are kept, and where to find certain ingredients.

Wash your hands

It is important to keep your hands clean when you are cooking, so be sure to wash them often with warm soapy water. It may be tempting to taste all the delicious food you are making especially if you get it on your hands, but do not lick them (or the spoon)! You should never taste uncooked food or food that has raw eggs in it.

Keep food separate

Keep uncooked food away from cooked food, and wash off any utensils that you have used during one stage of your cooking before moving on to another. Cleaning the utensils after working with meat or eggs is especially important, and this should be done straight away.

Tie back your hair

Finding hair in your food is gross so keep your hair fastened and out of the way. It is also a good idea to make sure you do not have any loose-fitting clothes on that could get in the way of your cooking. Wear an apron to keep you clean and shoes to protect your feet in case hot food or liquid spills.

Prepare

Read the recipe properly before you begin cooking. Prepare the ingredients and tools you will be using to cook, and set them out so you know where everything is and when you will be using them. Make sure you understand the instructions before starting and ask an adult to help you.

Be careful around knives

The knives are sharp. Please be careful when working with them. A good idea is to practice with them first with an adult to help you. Make sure that they are placed somewhere safe and never with the sharp point facing anyone. I know I said to clean up as you go along, but please do not put knives into a sink of soapy water; someone may stick their hand in there and get cut. The same rule applies to any other sharp tool that you will be working with.

Fire

If a fire starts, the first thing to do is call an adult. You should never put water on a fire. If the flames are large, leave the area immediately. If the fire is small, an adult can use baking soda to extinguish it, and if it is inside a pan, they can put a lid on it.

Oven gloves

Have a good-fitting pair of oven gloves available for you to use. Use these when working around the oven and hot pots and pans. Be mindful of the steamer and do not get into direct contact with the steam as this could burn you.

Turn everything off

Turn off the stove and unplug all appliances when you are done. If you are still cooking, remember not to leave any food unattended; if you need to leave the room, ask someone to watch the food for you.

8
Let's Cook!

Here we are: the part of the book that you have been waiting for—the recipes.

Each of the recipes will follow three main steps to complete before you end up with an amazing meal:

- Prepare the ingredients

- Prepare your cooking tools

- Cook

By preparing your ingredients before you start cooking, you save a lot of time and make sure that you have everything you need before you get started. You do not want to realize halfway through a recipe that you are missing an important ingredient. So start with the list of ingredients that each recipe provides for you, and prepare them according to the instructions. Chop, grate, wash, and measure as you need to. Being organized will make cooking so much easier and fun.

Take out what you will need to cook with which can include knives, spoons, steamers, pots, or cutting boards. Organize everything you will need just like you did with the ingredients.

Finally, you can start cooking, but before we get to that part, I want to give you four last important pieces of kitchen advice.

Read carefully

Recipes can be tricky as there is often a lot going on at the same time, and the directions may be a bit confusing at times. You and a grown-up should sit down and go through the recipe carefully. There will be a lot of new words (we will call this "lingo") that may need to be explained to you.

Once you are comfortable in the kitchen and have some experience with cooking, you can begin to experiment with recipes, but for now, follow them as directed. Once you get the original recipes right, you can then get creative with them.

Pay attention

It is important to be focused when working in the kitchen. You are working with heat and sharp tools which can be dangerous. Keep an eye on your food while it cooks, and be aware of any timers you have going that are keeping track of cooking times.

Be sure to pay attention to measurements. Cooking is a science, and often we need to stick to the correct measurements to ensure that our food comes out successfully. Too much salt or too little water can make or break a recipe.

Be safe

Remember our rules from the previous chapter? Give them a read-over every time you are about to cook so you remember how to stay safe when cooking.

Make mistakes

It is okay to make mistakes and I am very sure you will be making many. I still do and I have been cooking for years. We learn from our mistakes, and mistakes are an important part of the learning process.

9
Recipes

Steamed Pork Shaomai (or Shumai or Siuai)

There are various different spellings for steamed shaomai based on which region you are from, but they all refer to the same dish which is steamed pork dumplings.

This dish can also be made with shrimp, and I have even seen vegetarian and vegan versions of this dish which are made with mushrooms.

Time: 40 minutes

Serving Size: 5 servings

Prep Time: 20 minutes

Cook Time: 20 minutes

Ingredients:

- 20 circular egg dumpling wrappers
- 3 shitake mushrooms that have been soaked and finely chopped
- 2 slices of grated ginger
- 2 finely chopped scallions
- 2 tsp oyster sauce
- frozen peas (optional)
- 1 ¼ tsp sugar
- ¼ tsp white pepper
- ¼ tsp salt
- ½ tsp oil
- 1 tbsp Shaoxing wine
- 1 tbsp light soy sauce

- 3 tbsp water

- 1 tsp sesame oil

- 1 tsp cornstarch

- 8 oz of peeled, deveined, and roughly chopped shrimp

- 10 oz ground pork

Utensils:

- mixing bowls and spoon

- a bowl of water

- measuring cups and spoons

- chopping knife and board

- bamboo steamer (or alternative)

- dumpling steamer liners

- a pot

- grater

- food processor

Directions:

1. We will start by making the filling. Mix the sugar, white pepper, cornstarch, Shaoxing wine, soy sauce, water, and sesame oil with the pork. Stir in a clockwise direction for about 5 minutes. It should look like a fine paste.

2. Take the second bowl and mix the shrimp with the oil and the salt. Place both bowls in the fridge as you prepare the rest of the ingredients.

3. Grate the ginger.

4. Finely chop the scallions and shitake mushrooms. Be careful of the sharp knife! If you need some help, ask an adult to lend you a hand.

5. Add the scallions, ginger, mushrooms, shrimp, and pork mixture to one large bowl.

6. Add the oyster sauce.

7. Stir the mixture again for 5 minutes in one direction. This can also be done in a food processor.

8. Line your steamer with your dumpling steamer liner.

9. Now, we are going to assemble the shaomai by forming a circle with the fingers of your non-dominant hand—so if you are left-handed, you will use your right hand, and if you are right-handed, you will use your left hand.

10. Gently press down on the middle of the wrapper so you create a little bowl where the mixture can sit.

11. It needs to be just right—not too deep that you cannot fold over the edges and not too shallow that a teaspoon and a half of filling won't fit.

12. Place about 1 ½ teaspoons of the filling in the middle of the dumpling wrapper and gently push the mixture down to create a clean top.

13. Dip your fingers into your bowl of water and turn the sides of the wrapper onto the top of the dumpling. You may need to wet your fingers again.

14. If you have decided to use peas, you can add them to the top of the shaomai as garnish.

15. Ask an adult to help you set up your bamboo steamer in your wok or pot with about half an inch of water or just enough to come up to the bottom rim. It is important that the steamer is always in the water.

16. Place the shaomai in the steamer. They need to be about an inch apart.

17. Using medium to high heat, steam the shaomai for 12 minutes.

18. Enjoy!

Har Gow or Shrimp Dumplings

This is a very popular dim sum dish, and waiters are often rushing around to get these dumplings out to hungry customers.

In this recipe, we are going to make our own dough as well as the filling.

Time: 1 hour 20 minutes

Serving Size: 6 servings

Prep Time: 1 hour

Cook Time: 20 minutes

Ingredients for the Filling:

- ¼ tsp white pepper
- ¼ tsp salt
- ½ tsp minced ginger
- 1 tsp sugar
- 1 tsp oyster sauce
- 1 tsp sesame oil
- 1 tbsp vegetable oil
- ½ cup finely chopped bamboo shoots
- ½ lb deveined and peeled raw shrimp that has been patted dry

Ingredients for the Dough:

- 3 tsp lard or oil
- ½ cup cornstarch or tapioca starch
- 1 cup wheat starch
- 1 ¼ cups boiling water

Utensils:

- mixing bowls and spoons
- measuring cups and spoons
- damp paper towel

- kitchen scale
- rolling pin
- bamboo steamer
- bowl of water

Directions:

1. We will begin with the filling by mixing the white pepper, salt, ginger, sesame oil, sugar, oyster sauce, oil, and shrimp together in a mixing bowl.

2. We want the mixture to look sticky so whip the ingredients until it does.

3. Add the chopped bamboo shoots.

4. Cover the mixture and place it in the fridge while we prepare the dough.

5. In a mixing bowl, mix together the cornstarch and the wheat starch.

6. Carefully pour the boiling water. While you or an adult is pouring the water, the second person will be whisking the mixture to form a clear dough.

7. Continue to stir as you add the lard and oil.

8. Begin to knead the dough, but make sure it is not too hot! You want the dough to turn into a smooth ball.

9. Roll the dough out so it becomes a long cylinder.

10. Divide the cylinder into 18 pieces which should weigh about 0.8 ounces each. You can use a digital scale.

11. To keep the dough moist and easy to work with, cover it with a damp

paper towel.

12. Test the dough by taking one of the pieces and rolling it out into a shape like a finger.

13. You want it to form quickly without any cracking or stickiness.

14. We are now going to make the dumplings, so turn on the stove and set up your steamer.

15. Using a rolling pin, roll out the pieces of dough into 3-inch circles and place them under a damp paper towel to keep them moist and easy to work with.

16. We are going to fold the dumplings using a simple half-moon technique.

17. First, wet your fingers with water.

18. Now wet the outer edges of the wrapper but only half of the wrapper. Think of it as a semicircle.

19. Put a tablespoon of filling in the middle of the wrapper.

20. Fold it in half.

21. Press the edges together so that you create a strong seal. We don't want any of the filling falling out.

22. To make the dumpling sit upright, use your palm to gently flatten the bottom.

23. Well done! You have a dumpling. Continue folding.

24. The water in the steamer should be boiling by now, and it is time to start steaming the dumplings. Add them to the steamer leaving some space

for them to expand.

25. Using high heat, steam them for 6 minutes.

26. Serve them hot and enjoy!

Tips and Notes:

- If you live in a drier climate, add 1–2 teaspoons more water.
- The water for the dough must be boiling hot.
- If you do not have pork lard, you can use oil.

Char Siu Bao or Steamed Barbecue Pork Buns

As hard as I try, I cannot resist a char siu bao—soft, fluffy, and stuffed with a delicious filling.

For this recipe, we will be making the dough ourselves. This process is super interesting and fun to do. It's exactly like being in a science lab doing experiments except we are in our kitchen cooking.

Time: 3 hours 30 minutes

Serving Size: 10 buns

CHINESE DIM SUM COOKBOOK FOR KIDS

Prep Time: 3 hours

Cook Time: 30 minutes

Ingredients for the Dough:

- 1 tsp active dry yeast
- 1–2 tsp water (optional)
- 2 ½ tsp baking powder
- 5 tbsp sugar
- ¼ cup canola or vegetable oil
- ¾ cup warm water
- 1 cup cornstarch
- 2 cups all-purpose flour
- Ingredients for the Filling:
- 2 tbsp all-purpose flour
- ⅓ cup shallots or red onion
- 2 tsp sesame oil
- 2 tsp dark soy sauce
- 1 tbsp sugar
- 1 tbsp light soy sauce
- 1 ½ tbsp oyster sauce

- ½ cup chicken stock

- 1 ½ cups diced Chinese roast pork (either store-bought or homemade)

Utensils:

- mixing bowls and spoon

- electric mixer (or you can use a bowl and knead by hand)

- sieve

- measuring cups and spoons

- bamboo steamer

- wok

- bowl of water

- damp cloth

- parchment paper cut into 4x4-inch squares

Directions:

1. In a mixing bowl, mix the yeast with the warm water so it dissolves.

2. Sieve the flour and cornstarch and add them to the yeast and water.

3. Add the sugar and oil.

4. If you are using an electric mixer, turn it on to its lowest setting until a smooth dough ball is formed. If you are using your hands, knead the dough instead.

5. Cover the dough with a damp cloth. Let it sit for 2 hours.

6. Now we will make the meat filling while the dough rests.

7. Place the wok over medium heat and heat up the oil.

8. When the oil has been heated up, add the onions and stir-fry them for a minute.

9. Now you can add in the light and dark soy sauces along with the sesame oil, oyster sauce, and sugar.

10. Turn the heat down to a medium-low.

11. Keep stirring until it begins to bubble then add the chicken stock and flour.

12. After a couple of minutes, it should begin to thicken and you can remove it from the heat.

13. Now you can add the roast pork and set it aside to cool as we return to the dough.

14. Once your dough has rested, you can add the baking powder and turn the mixer to its lowest setting.

15. How is the dough looking? Is it dry? If it is, then add 1–2 teaspoons of water.

16. Knead the dough until it becomes smooth again, cover it with the damp cloth, and leave it for 15 minutes.

17. While the dough is resting, grab your parchment paper and cut it into 10 4x4-inch squares.

18. You can now begin to prepare your steamer so bring the water to a boil.

19. We need 10 equal pieces of dough, so roll the dough into one long piece and divide it up equally.

20. Press each piece of dough into a flat circular shape. It should be thicker in the center than the outside and about 4 ½ inches big.

21. Time to fold our buns which can be done in numerous ways. Feel free to fold your bao how you please; this is a good time to practice. I am going to use a simple fold and pleat the top of the buns.

22. Put some filling into the middle of your wrappers and gather the edges up to wrap around the filling. Pinch the folds so you create some pleats.

23. Hold the dough in both of your hands and move your hands in a circular motion. We want the bun to become taller as we do not want them to expand outward.

24. Put your buns on the parchment paper, and when your steamer has been set up, begin to steam them in batches.

25. Each batch should be steamed over high heat for about 12 minutes.

26. Enjoy!

Tips and Notes:

- Make sure that you pre-boil the water in the steamer. This is the trick to getting them to rise quickly and crack open at the top. Science is cool!

Youtiao or Chinese Fried Dough Sticks

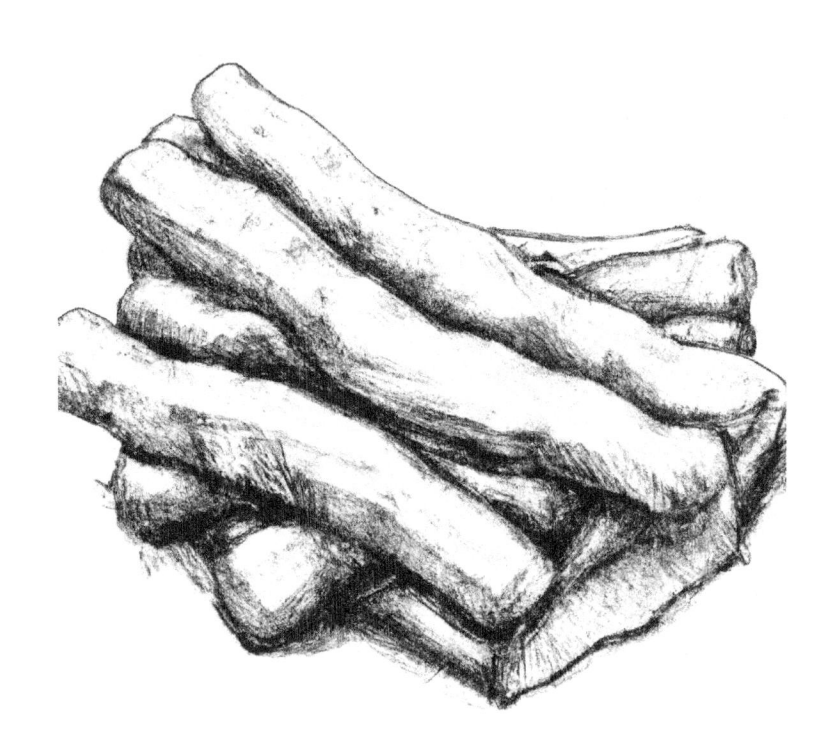

This breakfast favorite is also known as Chinese crullers.

These are very irresistible dim sum and are usually served with soy milk, pancakes, and porridge and, as you will see in the next recipe, can be incorporated as an ingredient in other dishes.

This recipe will teach you patience as the preparation time is very long—12 hours to be exact.

Time: 12 hours 20 minutes

Serving Size: 10 crullers

Prep Time: 12 hours

Cook Time: 20 minutes

Ingredients:

- ½ tsp salt
- 1 ½ tsp baking powder
- 1 tbsp milk
- 2 tbsp softened unsalted butter
- about ⅓ cup water
- 2 cups all-purpose flour
- 1 egg
- oil for frying

Utensils:

- mixing bowl and spoon
- measuring cups and spoons
- electric mixer
- plastic wrap
- wok
- chopsticks or tongs

Directions:

1. Add the flour, salt, baking powder, milk, softened butter, and egg to a mixing bowl, and using your electric mixer, mix the ingredients together on the lowest setting.

2. Slowly pour in the water. Do this in batches as the amount of water you may need will vary depending on the humidity level.

3. You want the dough to be sticky but not stuck to the sides of the bowl, so knead the dough for 15 minutes. If you do not have an electric mixer, you can use your hands, but add 5–10 minutes to the kneading time.

4. Take the dough and begin to form it into a loaf shape that is ¼-inch thick and 4 inches wide. You really want it to be even and the same all the way around.

5. Place your piece of plastic wrap on the middle of a baking sheet or plate. Place your formed dough in the middle of the plastic and wrap it completely around the dough.

6. Pop it into the fridge and leave it overnight.

7. We can begin to work with the dough again once it has reached room temperature and is very soft to the touch. In the morning, take it out of the fridge and let it sit on the counter for about 1–3 hours. Keep it wrapped in plastic.

8. Turn on the stove to medium heat and heat up the oil in the wok. It should be around 400–425 °F.

9. Peel the plastic wrap off the dough and then cover it very lightly in flour.

10. Slice the dough into 1-inch wide pieces then stack them two by two.

11. Using a chopstick, press the center lengthwise then hold the ends of each piece and pull the dough so it turns into a rope about 9 inches long.

12. Ask an adult to help you lower the dough into the wok. The dough should rise to the surface straightaway. Roll the dough around in the oil so it cooks evenly; this should take about 1 minute.

13. Once the dough turns a light golden brown, they are done. Do not over-fry them as they will become too crunchy.

14. Cook the remaining dough.

15. Enjoy!

Tips and Notes:

- The amount of water you use will vary depending on the humidity in your area. The dough should not stick to the bowl.

Zhaliang or Fried Dough Rice Noodle Rolls

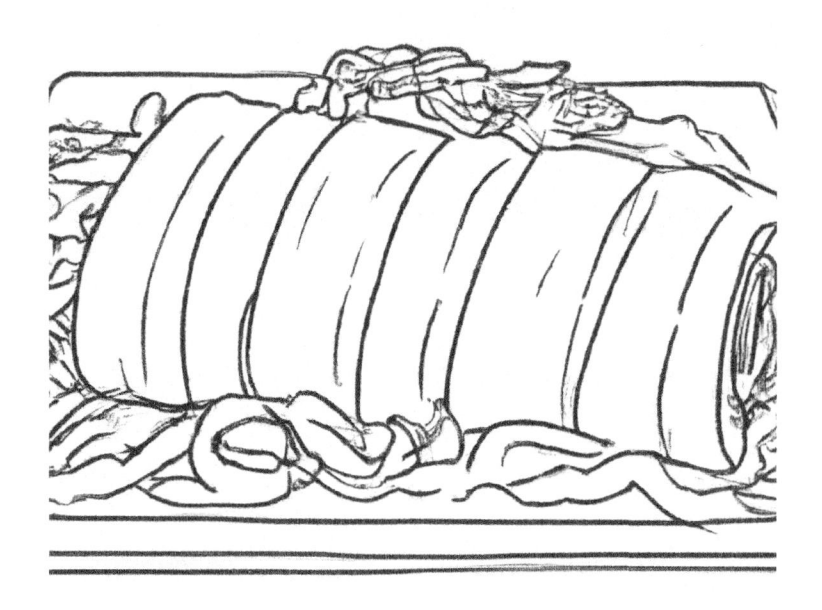

I believe that this is a firm favorite among kids. Zhaliang is silky rice noodles that have been wrapped around a crispy fried dough. This creates a very interesting taste experience because of the difference between the soft and crunchy parts.

The zhaliang is usually drizzled with sweet soy sauce which just adds to its delicious flavor.

Time: 1 hour

Serving Size: 6 servings

Prep Time: 30 minutes

Cook Time: 30 minutes

Ingredients for the Sauce:

- 1 tsp oyster sauce
- 1 tsp oil
- 2 tsp dark soy sauce
- 5 tsp sugar
- 2 ½ tbsp light soy sauce
- ⅓ cup water
- 1 scallion (the white part only)
- 1-inch piece of ginger
- salt to taste
- Ingredients for the Zhaliang:
- 1 youtiao also known as a Chinese fried dough stick
- ¼ tsp salt
- 1 tbsp mung bean starch
- 2 tbsp wheat starch
- 2 tbsp cornstarch
- 5 tbsp rice flour
- 1 cup water

- vegetable or canola oil for brushing

Utensils:

- mixing bowls and spoons
- large flat plate
- pan
- wok with a lid
- a metal pan that can fit in your wok and float on simmering water (I used a 9x13-inch nonstick sheet pan)
- dough scraper
- pastry brush
- new 100% cotton cloth in a natural color like white
- oven gloves or plate gripper

Directions:

1. Before we begin, preheat your oven to 350 °F.
2. We will be making the sauce first, so please place a pot on the stovetop on medium heat.
3. Add all the ingredients for the sauce and heat it until it begins to gently bubble.
4. Let it cool and remove the scallion and the ginger.
5. Now for the youtiao, break it apart lengthwise so you are left with two

long pieces.

6. Warm-up these pieces in the oven for 5–8 minutes. You want them to be warm and crunchy, but make sure they don't get too crisp.

7. Now we will prepare the rice noodles by mixing together the rice flour, mung bean starch, wheat starch, cornstarch, and salt in a large mixing bowl.

8. Dissolve the dry ingredients by slowly adding the water to the bowl and stirring. Stir for about 3 minutes.

9. Put the bowl on the side and let the air bubbles disappear.

10. Take the cotton cloth and dip it into some water so that it is completely soaked.

11. Prepare your assembly station by coating a large plate with oil.

12. Pre-boil some water in your wok as we prepare to cook the rice noodles.

13. Line your metal pan with the wet cloth. Do not wring out any of the water, keep it soaked.

14. Take your water and starch mixture and give it a stir.

15. Pour just enough mixture into the pan so that the bottom is covered. Do not make it too thick or your noodles will be thick.

16. You will need to work fast here so get an adult to help you.

17. Your water should be boiling now, so ask an adult to lower the pan into the wok carefully.

18. The pan needs to be level, not too high on either side, or the noodles will

be too thick on one side and too thin on the other.

19. Place the lid on the wok and steam the noodles for 2 minutes.

20. After 2 minutes, take the pan out of the wok.

21. Now assemble the zhaliang by carefully taking the cloth out of the pan. This must be done while the cloth and noodles are still hot, so let an adult do this as well.

22. Place the cloth noodle-side down onto the oiled plate.

23. Carefully remove the noodle from the cloth using your hands and the dough scraper. The noodle should remain on the plate.

24. Place the youtiao on the noodle and roll it up.

25. Cut it up into bite-sized pieces and place them on a serving plate.

26. Serve with a drizzle of the sauce and enjoy!

Tips and notes:

- The sauce can be kept in the fridge for 2 weeks.

- Rinse the cloth out in clean water before making the second noodle.

Dim Sum-Style Gai Lan or Chinese Broccoli

This special Chinese broccoli is related to the traditional broccoli florets that you find in most grocery stores. They belong to the same family.

This is a very simple and common way to prepare and serve this vegetable. Often, when visiting a dim sum restaurant, this is the only green dish you will find on the cart.

Time: 30 minutes

Serving Size: 4 servings

Prep Time: 25 minutes

Cook Time: 5 minutes

Ingredients:

- 1 lb Chinese broccoli
- 1 tsp salt
- 1-2 tbsp vegetable oil
- 2-3 tbsp oyster sauce
- 8 cups water

Utensils:

- measuring cups and spoons
- colander
- wok or large pot
- tongs or chopsticks
- plate

Directions:

1. First, you must wash the Chinese broccoli very well before cooking. See the notes for instructions. In a large pot or a wok, bring the water to a boil and add the salt.

2. When the water is boiling (we want it to have big bubbles), carefully lower your broccoli into the pot. You can do this in two batches if you have quite a lot of broccoli.

3. Using your tongs or chopsticks, carefully push the broccoli under the water so that it is completely covered. You want them to be tender but still crunchy, and this will take about 1–2 minutes to achieve.

4. Remove your broccoli when they are cooked to your liking.

5. Shake off any water and place the broccoli on a plate.

6. Using a tablespoon, splash some oyster sauce onto your vegetables.

7. Enjoy!

Notes and Tips:

- Wash the Chinese broccoli by submerging it in a basin of cold water and gently massaging them with your hands to remove sand or dirt. Leave it in the water for about 5 minutes. Put the broccoli into a colander, clean out the basin and refill it with water. You will repeat this process two more times.

Chinese Wu Tao Gou or Taro Cake

Taro Cake is a dim sum treat that is usually eaten to celebrate the Lunar New Year. It is made out of taro root which is a vegetable that can be compared to the potato. It certainly is an interesting ingredient to make a cake with, but the beauty of the taro is that it works so well in savory and sweet dishes. This is what makes it such a popular ingredient.

Time: 1 hour 30 minutes

Serving Size: 12 cakes

Prep Time: 45 minutes

Cook Time: 45 minutes

Ingredients:

- 1 tsp white pepper powder
- 2 tsp sesame oil
- 3 tbsp oil
- ½ cup roughly chopped dried shrimp (optional)
- 1 cup glutinous rice flour also known as sweet rice flour
- 2 ½ cups rice flour
- 4 cups water (divided)
- 3 links of Chinese sausage cut into bite-size pieces
- 8 chopped scallions
- 2 lb of taro cut into ½-inch cubes

Utensils:

- measuring cups and spoons
- mixing bowl and spoon
- wok
- metal spatula
- knife and chopping board
- two 9-inch round cake pans

- bamboo steamer

Directions:

1. Fry the Chinese sausage in the wok over medium heat for 2 minutes.

2. Add the dried shrimp and fry for a further minute.

3. Continue to fry, adding the taro and scallions. You will fry this for an additional 3 minutes.

4. Add the salt, white pepper, and sesame oil.

5. Submerge all the ingredients in 2 ½ cups of water.

6. Place a lid over the wok and simmer for 8 minutes over medium heat.

7. Turn down the heat, uncover the wok, and let the taro cakes cool.

8. In your large mixing bowl, add the two different types of flour and the remaining 1 ½ cups of water. Combine them well.

9. Add the taro mixture and stir well. You want the mixture to form a thick paste.

10. Coat your two cake pans with oil.

11. Halve your taro cake mixture and add it to the cake pans.

12. For 45 minutes, steam the pans. You may need to do this one pan at a time. Make sure you do not burn your bamboo steamer by letting the water run out during steaming. Top the water up every 10 minutes or so.

13. After 45 minutes, test to see if your cakes are done by inserting a toothpick into the middle. If it comes out clean, it is done.

14. Let the cakes cool completely, and if you are planning on freezing them, you can pop them into a ziplock bag and leave them in the freezer.

15. If you want to eat them now, slice the cakes into rectangles and pan-fry them until they are crispy and brown.

16. Sprinkle salt over them and serve.

17. Enjoy!

Notes and Tips:

- You can substitute 4 ounces of bacon for Chinese sausage.

Easy-Peasy Steamed Ribs in Black Bean Sauce

Steamed ribs in black bean sauce is one of my favorite recipes to make, and I find it to also be one of the easiest. I have fond memories of searching for this dish among the carts exiting the restaurant kitchen when I was out with my parents for yum cha.

Now, you can make this popular dish at home with me.

Time: 25 minutes

Serving Size: 6 servings

Prep Time: 15 minutes

RECIPES

Cook Time: 10 minutes

Ingredients:

- ½ tsp salt
- 1 ½ tsp potato starch
- 3 tsp black bean garlic sauce
- 1 tbsp chicken bouillon powder
- 1 tbsp sugar
- 2.2 lb pork spareribs

Utensils

- mixing bowl and spoon
- measuring cups and spoons
- knife and cutting board
- wok
- bamboo steamer

Directions:

1. Set up your steamer.

2. Ask an adult to help you cut your ribs into small pieces that are about 0.6 inches thick. Make sure that when you cut your pieces, there is enough meat on either side.

3. Mix the salt, sugar, potato starch, cooking oil, chicken bouillon powder,

and garlic sauce together in a mixing bowl.

4. Add the ribs, coat well, and let them marinate for 20 minutes.

5. Once it has marinated, steam the pork on high for 10 minutes. This will give you the same type of ribs that you get from dim sum restaurants.

6. If you want more tender ribs, you can steam the ribs for up to an hour or longer.

7. Enjoy!

Notes and Tips:

- Leave the pork out for 20 minutes prior to cooking. The pork should be cooked when it is at room temperature as meat tends to be tough if cooked cold (Ta, 2021).

- The fattier the pieces of meat, the more succulent they will be.

RECIPES 77

Chicken Spring Rolls

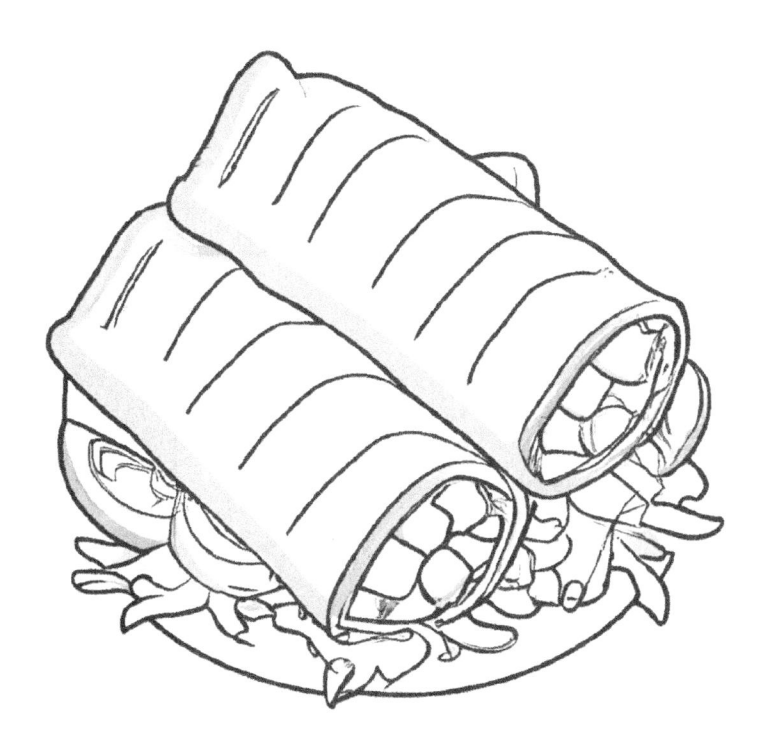

Crispy spring rolls are a delight to bite into. One, two, three, four bites, and it's done and filling you up as you reach for another.

Time: 1 hour 20 minutes

Serving Size: 50 rolls

Prep Time: 1 hour

Cook Time: 20 minutes

Ingredients:

- ¼ tsp freshly ground black pepper

- 1 tsp rice wine or white wine
- 1 tsp cornstarch
- 1 tsp fresh grated ginger
- 1 tbsp soy sauce
- 2 tbsp cooking oil
- 2 tbsp oyster sauce
- 2 cups cooking oil for frying
- 1–2 stalks of green onion, chopped
- 2 cloves of garlic, minced
- 2 carrots chopped finely into julienne strips
- ½ head of a small cabbage, shredded
- 50 spring roll wrappers
- 1 lb ground chicken

Ingredients for the Paste:

- 1 tbsp cornstarch
- ¼ cup water

Utensils:

- mixing bowl and spoon
- measuring cups and spoons

RECIPES

- wok
- metal spatula
- cooling rack
- paper towel
- baking sheet
- plastic wrap

Directions:

1. Begin by adding the wine, pepper, cornstarch, and soy sauce to a large mixing bowl. Mix well.

2. Add the chicken and let it marinate for 10 minutes.

3. Ask an adult to turn on the stove too high and heat up your wok.

4. When the wok is hot, add 1 tablespoon of the cooking oil. Get an adult to help you do this.

5. Add the chicken and stir-fry until it has browned. Then remove it from the pan and place it in a bowl.

6. Reduce the heat to medium and wipe down the wok with a paper towel.

7. Add the remaining tablespoon of oil, green onion, garlic, and ginger. Cook for 30 seconds; you do not want to burn it.

8. Stir in the cabbage and carrots and turn the heat up to medium-high.

9. Stir-fry for 2 minutes or until the carrots become soft.

10. Add the chicken back to the wok along with the oyster sauce and stir well.

11. Cool the mixture on a baking sheet, propping one side up so that the liquid collects on one side.

12. You can throw away the liquid once the mixture has been cooled.

13. Now we will create the paste to seal the spring rolls.

14. Whip together the cornstarch and water to create a paste.

Folding the Spring Rolls:

1. Place the spring roll wrapper so that a corner is facing you.

2. Spoon some of the mixture about 2 inches away from the corner that is closest to you. You should use about a tablespoon of the mixture; you do not want to overstuff it.

3. Roll it over once and fold over both sides. It is very similar to rolling a burrito.

4. Continue to roll it into a cylinder. It should look like an envelope.

5. Using your finger, smear some of the cornstarch paste onto the corner that is furthest away from you and seal the spring roll.

6. Continue to roll up the rest of your spring rolls and place them seam-side down on a baking pan ready to be fried. Cover them with plastic wrap to prevent them from drying out.

Frying the Spring Rolls:

1. An adult can help you heat the oil in a wok.

2. Slowly slide in the spring rolls and turn them often to cook them evenly.

3. Remove the spring rolls when they are golden brown.

4. Using the rack, drain the excess oil off the spring rolls.

5. Enjoy!

Notes and Tips:

- You can use pork, beef, or turkey for this recipe.

- Make sure your mixture is cooled down before you roll your spring rolls; otherwise, the wrappers will become soggy.

- Make sure you remove most of the liquid from the mixture as this will also make the rolls soggy.

- If you would like to freeze your spring rolls, put them into a freezer bag ensuring it is not overpacked, and freeze them.

- When you would like to eat the frozen spring rolls, you can pop them in a frying pan and cook them from frozen. If you defrost them, they will be soggy and soft.

- When reheating leftover cooked spring rolls, do so in an oven at 300 °F for 5–7 minutes or until they are crispy.

Ngao Yuk or Cantonese Steamed Beef Balls

Want to throw some beef mince around? This is a fun and pretty simple recipe, but it does have a long preparation time, so keep that in mind if you decide to make it. Once the basics are prepped, the recipe itself is quite quick.

Time: 28 minutes

Serving Size: 16–20 servings

Prep Time: 20 minutes

Cook Time: 8 minutes

Ingredients:

- 1 pinch of baking soda
- 1 pinch of white pepper
- 4 drops of sesame oil
- ¼ tsp salt
- ⅓ tsp dried citrus peel
- ½ tsp chicken bouillon
- ½ tsp sugar
- 1 tsp oyster sauce
- 2 tsp vegetable oil
- 3 tsp cornstarch
- ½ cup cold water
- 1 bunch watercress
- 1 lb ground beef

Utensils:

- mixing bowl and spoon
- measuring cups and spoons
- knife and cutting board
- bamboo steamer

- wok

Directions:

1. Mix the baking soda into the mince and leave it in the fridge for 3–4 hours.

2. Soften the citrus peel in warm water, drain, and then mince.

3. Using your hands, form a ball with the mince.

4. Now the fun bit—take your mince ball and throw it back into the bowl. Do this about 10–15 times. This will help the beef stick together and make sure it does not crumble when cooked.

5. Prepare the cornstarch by adding it to cold water and stirring it well so it dissolves. Add this to the beef mixture.

6. Now add the sesame oil, chicken bouillon, sugar, salt, citrus peel, and white pepper.

7. Finally, add the oyster sauce.

8. It's time to get messy again. Use your hands to form beef balls; use about 2 tablespoons of beef.

9. Line your steamer with watercress and place the beef balls on top of it. Turn on the stove, and once the water starts boiling, begin timing. Steam for 8 minutes on high heat.

10. Enjoy!

Cantonese Fried Noodles

This is a quick meal that comes together in under 20 minutes. If you like chow mein or garlic noodles, you will love this dish. Not only is it very delicious, but the hidden vegetable makes it healthy as well. You can also use different ingredients which makes it very customizable.

Time: 30 minutes

Serving Size: 4–6 servings

Prep Time: 15 minutes

Cook Time: 15 minutes

Ingredients:

- ¼–½ tsp red pepper flakes
- ½ tsp salt
- 2 tsp sugar
- 2 tsp minced garlic
- 2 tsp oyster sauce
- 2 tbsp oil
- 2 tbsp plus 2 tsp toasted sesame oil
- ¼ cup low-sodium soy sauce
- 1 ½ cups mixed vegetables like shredded cabbage, carrots, and bean sprouts.
- 8 scallions
- 12 oz of Hong Kong-style egg noodles

Utensils:

- mixing bowl and spoon
- measuring cups and spoons
- large pot
- knife and cutting board
- colander

- wok

- large spatula

Directions:

1. Bring a pot of water to a boil.

2. While the pot is heating up, prepare the scallions by separating the white and green parts. Thinly julienne the scallions and set them aside.

3. Stir and combine the oyster and soy sauce, sugar, minced garlic, red pepper flakes, salt, and 1 teaspoon of sesame oil. Set the bowl aside.

4. Add the noodles to the water as soon as it begins to boil and cook them according to the package instructions.

5. Heat your wok or pan over high heat for several minutes. It needs to become very hot. Please make sure an adult is here to help you.

6. Carefully add 1 tablespoon of sesame oil and canola oil to the wok.

7. Add an even layer of noodles to the wok once it becomes hot again.

8. Carefully cover all the noodles in oil by swirling the pan.

9. Cook the noodles until they become crispy which should take between 4–5 minutes.

10. Using a spatula, flip over the noodles in batches. Add the remaining oil to the edges of the wok and swirl the pan around to coat the noodles again.

11. Continue to fry the noodles for another 3–5 minutes.

12. Heat the white part of the scallion for about 10 seconds in the remaining

1 teaspoon of oil. Add the carrots and let them sizzle for an additional 10 seconds.

13. Add the noodles and shredded cabbage.

14. Drizzle the soy sauce mixture over the noodles and toss for 1–2 minutes so the sauce covers all the noodles evenly.

15. Throw in the bean sprouts and the green parts of the scallion. Combine and serve warm.

16. Enjoy!

Tips and Notes:

- If your wok is not big enough for all the noodles, you can do them in two batches. You can use ½ tablespoon of sesame oil and ½ tablespoon of canola oil per batch or per side.

Pork and Vegetable Rice Noodle Rolls

Slippery steamed noodles with mince and vegetables. Are you ready to slurp it all up for supper? This is a really easy treat for adults and kids.

Time: 35 minutes

Serving Size: 4 servings

Prep Time: 15 minutes

Cook Time: 20 minutes

Ingredients for the Rolls:

- 1 tsp oil

- 1 tsp grated ginger
- 2 tsp fish sauce
- 1 tbsp brown sugar
- 1 tbsp soy sauce
- 2 tbsp oyster sauce
- 2 crushed cloves of garlic
- 2 finely sliced spring onions
- 1 diced celery stalk
- 1 diced carrot
- ½ diced red capsicum
- ½ diced zucchini
- 14 oz pork mince
- 14 oz fresh rice noodle sheets

Ingredients for the Sauce:

- 1 tsp sesame sauce
- 1 tsp kecap manis or Indonesian sweet soy sauce
- 1 tsp soy sauce
- 1 tsp white sugar
- 2 tsp rice wine vinegar

Utensils:

- mixing bowls and spoons

- measuring cups and spoons

- knife and cutting board

- dumpling steamer liners

- wok

- bamboo steamer

Directions:

1. Heat the oil in a wok, add your mince, and fry until it browns.

2. Drain off the excess liquid.

3. Add the ginger, garlic, and vegetables and cook for 2–3 minutes.

4. Now add the soy and oyster sauce as well as the sugar and cook until the sauce has thickened and the vegetables are tender. This should take about 3–4 minutes. Once done, set aside to cool.

5. Cut your rice noodle sheets into 3.5x5.5-inch pieces.

6. Place some of the fillings on a piece of your rice noodle and roll it up in a cylinder shape.

7. Line your steamer with a dumpling liner and set it up over a pan or wok and bring the water to a simmer.

8. Steam for 3–4 minutes until the noodles are soft.

9. Add all the sauce ingredients to a small mixing bowl and stir.

10. Drizzle the sauce over the rolls and enjoy!

Congee or Chinese Rice Porridge

Congee is not only a Cantonese staple, and versions of this easy meal can be found in Burma, Indonesia, Japan, and even in European countries.

It is so simple to make and provides a warm, hearty meal for all family members—young and old!

This is the simple base recipe and you can add whatever you like and have available.

Time: 2 hours 20 minutes

Serving Size: 6 servings

Prep Time: 35 minutes

Cook Time: 1 hour 45 minutes

Ingredients:

- 1 tsp salt
- ¾ cup long-grain rice
- 8 cups water (or chicken, vegetable, or beef stock)

Optional Ingredients:

- minced ginger
- minced garlic
- lotus root
- ginkgo nuts
- shredded chicken
- shredded pork
- bok choy
- soft-boiled egg
- chopped peanuts

Utensils:

- mixing bowl and spoon
- measuring cups and spoons

- large pot

- sieve

Directions:

1. Rinse the rice in water and let it soak for 30 minutes.

2. Drain the water.

3. Using your large pot, bring the water or stock and rice to a boil.

4. Once it has started boiling, lower the heat to medium-low and place the lid on top. Keep the lid slightly open to help the steam escape.

5. Stir occasionally and continue to cook the rice until it becomes thick and creamy like porridge. This process can take anywhere from 1 ½ hours to 1 ¾ hours, so keep an eye on it.

6. Add salt to taste and remove from the stove.

7. Top with any additional toppings you prefer.

8. Enjoy!

Tips and Notes:

- Leftover congee can be refrigerated in a sealed container for up to 5 days.

- You can top your congee with anything. The optional ingredients listed are some of the more popular variations. You could also make congee sweet by adding sugar, dates, or raisins.

Yu Choy or Chinese Greens Stir-Fry

My parents would always tell me to "eat your greens." This is one way to make them happy. Chinese greens are known as yu choy, and they look quite similar to Chinese broccoli except that the stalks are thinner.

This is a really quick dish to make and goes well with many other dim sum dishes.

Time: 8 minutes

Serving Size: 4 servings

Prep Time: 3 minutes

Cook Time: 5 minutes

Ingredients:

- 1 tbsp oil
- 4–6 whole cloves of garlic
- ¼ cup vegetable or chicken broth
- 1 lb of Chinese greens cut into 3-inch lengths

Utensils:

- chopping board and knife
- wok
- metal spatula

Directions:

1. In your wok, heat the oil at a medium to medium-high temperature.
2. Add the whole garlic cloves and fry until they turn golden brown. Be careful not to burn them.
3. Add the Chinese greens, coating each stalk in the oil.
4. Add the broth and cover with a lid.
5. Keep covered for around 3 minutes until the stalks are soft but still have a crunch. They should still be bright green.
6. Enjoy!

Chicken Pot Stickers or Dumplings

Do you know what comfort food is? It is food that makes you feel good inside, and it is usually food that brings up certain memories of places or people.

Pot stickers are my comfort food. What are yours?

Time: 30 minutes

Serving Size: 4 servings

Prep Time: 20 minutes

Cook Time: 10 minutes

Ingredients:

- 1 tsp grated ginger
- 2 tbsp finely chopped coriander
- 2–3 tbsp vegetable oil
- 2 finely sliced green onions
- ½ cup chicken stock
- 12-round wonton wrappers
- 8.8 oz chicken mince
- soy sauce

Utensils:

- mixing bowl and spoon
- measuring cups and spoon
- fork
- brush
- wok

Directions:

1. In your bowl, mix together the mince, ginger, coriander, and green onions.

2. Lay out your wonton wrappers and add a tablespoon of the mixture to the middle of them. Brush the edges of the wrapper with water and fold

them over then seal them tightly by using your fork to press down the edges.

3. Heat up your wok and oil over medium-high heat.

4. Carefully lower the dumplings and cook each side for about a minute. They should look golden brown.

5. Add the stock to the pan and cover it with a lid.

6. Turn down the temperature and cook for another 5 minutes.

7. Serve with a little soy sauce and enjoy!

Chicken Dumpling Soup

Here, we have delicious chicken dumplings that are swimming around in a warm broth.

Time: 30 minutes

Serving Size: 6 servings

Prep Time: 20 minutes

Cook Time: 10 minutes

Ingredients:

- 1 tsp salt

- 1 tsp minced ginger
- 1 tbsp soy sauce
- 2 tbsp chopped chives
- 4–5 chopped button mushrooms
- 1 cup shredded savoy cabbage
- 2 cups water
- 2 cups chicken stock
- 1 packet of wonton skins
- 12 oz chicken mince

Utensils:

- mixing bowl and spoon
- measuring cups and spoons
- cutting board and knife
- food processor
- pot and lid
- slotted spoon

Directions:

1. Using your food processor, process ginger, chives, mushroom, and chives.

2. Add the salt and chicken mince and process it for 3–4 seconds.

3. Prepare your wonton skins by laying them out on a flat working surface and placing a tablespoon of the mixture in the middle.

4. Use your fingers and wet the edges of the skins to make them stick.

5. Take the edges and pull them together at the top of the wonton, squeeze them tightly, and twist to seal.

6. Use the rest of the mixture and create more dumplings.

7. Pour your stock, water, and soy sauce into a pan and bring it to a boil. When it is boiling, add your dumplings.

8. Simmer for 5 minutes, and once done, remove from the liquid with a slotted spoon.

9. Serve with the soup and enjoy!

Tips and Notes:

- You can chop the vegetables using a knife and chopping board should you not have a food processor.

Wonton Noodle Soup

Today, we are going to make our own chicken stock in preparation for this recipe. This is a very exciting process in cooking and healthier than buying your own. Stock can and is used in many recipes in this book so it is a useful skill to have.

Plus you can use the chicken in the Chicken Wonton Cups and Barbeque Chicken Dim Sim recipes coming up.

Time: 2 hours 15 minutes

Serving Size: 4 servings

Prep Time: 2 hours

Cook Time: 15 minutes

Ingredients:

- 1 tsp salt
- 1 tsp soy sauce
- 1 tsp dry sherry
- 1 tbsp vegetable stock powder
- 1 two-inch peeled and quartered pieces of fresh ginger
- 1 chopped onion
- 1 chopped carrot
- 2 sticks of chopped celery
- 1 bunch of roughly chopped bok choy
- 12–16 wontons or dumplings
- 1 lb rice noodles
- 4 lb organic chicken

Utensils:

- mixing bowl and spoon
- measuring cups and spoons
- large pot
- strainer

Directions:

1. Put the chicken in a large stockpot and cover it with water.

2. Add the stock powder, celery, carrot, onion, ginger, and salt, and let it come to a simmer.

3. Leave it to cook uncovered for 1–1 ½ hours.

4. Carefully take out the chicken, and using your sieve, strain the stock.

5. Add the soy sauce and the sherry and bring it to a simmer again.

6. Prepare the noodles as per the packet's instructions.

7. Cook the wontons or dumplings according to the package recommendations.

8. When they are almost ready, about 2 minutes left, add the bok choy and noodles to the stock.

9. Keep cooking until the wantons or dumplings are done.

10. Enjoy!

Chicken Wonton Cups

We are creating a fun eating experience today as you will get to build your own wonton cups!

Time: 30 minutes

Serving Size: 10 servings

Prep Time: 15 minutes

Cook Time: 15 minutes

Ingredients:

- 1 tsp honey

- 1 tsp lukewarm water
- 1 tsp toasted sesame seeds
- 2 tsp sweet soy sauce
- ½ peeled carrot, chopped into matchsticks
- 1 cucumber, halved and chopped into matchsticks
- 1 celery stick, halved and chopped into matchsticks
- 1 cup shredded iceberg lettuce
- 1 cup poached and thinly sliced chicken breast
- cooking spray

Utensils:

- mixing bowl and spoon
- measuring cups and spoons
- knife and chopping board
- muffin tin
- small serving bowls

Directions:

1. Preheat the oven to 360 °F

2. While the oven is heating, mix the sauce together by adding the honey, sweet soy, and water into a mixing bowl. Pour this over the shredded

chicken and then add the sesame seeds.

3. Spray each cup of the muffin tin with the cooking spray and line them with a wonton wrapper. Bake until they are golden which should take about 8 minutes.

4. Remove your cups and let them cool.

5. Place the rest of your vegetables in individual bowls and serve.

6. Get creative and build your wonton cups!

7. Enjoy!

Barbecued Chicken Dim Sum

I hate to waste food. It is important to be mindful of where our food comes from and how grateful we should be to have full tummies and a fridge full of food. This recipe uses leftover chicken, so if you have some in your fridge already (maybe you made some stock recently), you can use that.

This is also quite a spicy recipe, so be mindful of the chilies and leave them out if you prefer.

Time: 45 minutes

Serving Size: 8 servings

Prep Time: 30 minutes

Cook Time: 15 minutes

Ingredients:

- 5 tbsp toasted sesame seeds
- 5 tbsp barbeque sauce
- ½ bunch of fresh coriander
- ½-inch peeled and finely grated piece of ginger
- 1 lime
- 3 fresh chilies
- 4 spring onions
- 13 oz of light coconut milk or semi-skimmed milk
- 2 ½ cups of flour
- 10.5 oz of cooked chicken

Utensils:

1. mixing bowl and spoon
2. measuring cups and spoons
3. knife and chopping board
4. grater
5. wok or pot for steaming
6. bamboo steamer

7. food processor

8. parchment paper

Directions:

1. Deseed the chilies and then halve them. Trim and halve the spring onion.

2. Cut the spring onion and chilies lengthwise. Put them in a bowl of water and ice until they curl.

3. Chop the coriander and add the grated ginger, barbecue sauce, and a squeeze of lime juice. Add the shredded chicken and set aside.

4. Pulse the flour, coconut milk or semi-skimmed milk, and a pinch of salt in your food processor until it turns into a sticky dough.

5. Shape the dough into a sausage shape and cut it into 16 equal size pieces.

6. Flatten these pieces into circles.

7. Put equal amounts of your chicken mixture into the center of your circles leaving about a 1-inch gap around the edge.

8. Pull the sides over the edges and pinch together at the top to seal.

9. Prepare your steamer and bring some water to boil in your wok.

10. Cut out 12 pieces of parchment paper. They should be 4x4 inches, and place your dim sum on the paper, seal-side down.

11. Put them in the steamer, and once the water starts to boil, steam them for 12 minutes. They should be light, fluffy, and cooked through.

12. Remove the chilies and spring onion from the cold water and scatter them

on your dim sum. Sprinkle the sesame seeds over them and serve with hoisin sauce.

13. Enjoy!

Chive Pancakes

An easy-peasy savory pancake recipe that uses fresh chives as one of its main ingredients.

Time: 40 minutes

Serving Size: 3–4 servings

Prep Time: 10 minutes

Cook Time: 30 minutes

Ingredients:

- ½ tsp salt

- 1 tbsp oil

- 1 cup flour

- 1 cup water

- 1 bunch (about 2 cups) of trimmed chives cut into 1-inch long strips

- soy sauce

Utensils:

- mixing bowl and spoon

- measuring cups and spoons

- knife and cutting board

- nonstick frying pan

Directions:

1. In your mixing bowl, combine the flour and eggs. Slowly add the water and stir until it has been mixed well.

2. Add the chives and the salt.

3. Turn on your stove to medium heat and heat up the oil in your frying pan.

4. Use ⅓ of the batter to create your pancakes and cook for 4–5 minutes on each side.

5. Continue to cook your pancakes until the batter runs out.

6. Serve with soy sauce and enjoy!

Chinese Sausage and Sticky Rice

This recipe creates delicious domes of rice and is very easy to make. It is sure to become a must-have recipe on your home dim sum menu.

Time: 1 hour 15 minutes

Serving Size: 6 servings

Prep Time: 30 minutes

Cook Time: 45 minutes

Ingredients:

- ¼ tsp sesame oil

- ½ tsp salt
- 1 tsp Shaoxing wine
- 2 tsp dark soy sauce
- 1 tbsp oyster sauce
- 1 ½ tbsp soy sauce
- 2 tbsp oil
- ¼ cup chicken stock
- ¼ cup dried shrimp that has been soaked in warm water for 15 minutes
- 2 chopped scallions
- 1 medium finely diced onion
- 5 dried shitake mushrooms that have been softened in warm water and diced
- 3 links of Chinese sausages cut into discs
- 2 cups uncooked sticky rice
- white pepper to taste

Utensils:

- mixing bowl and spoon
- measuring cups and spoons
- knife and cutting board

- wok
- metal ladle

Directions:

1. Prepare the rice according to the instructions on the packet. Once cooked, let it cool.

2. In a small bowl, mix together the oyster and soy sauce, sesame oil, salt, and chicken stock.

3. Turn the stove to medium heat and heat up the oil.

4. Fry the shrimp for 30 seconds and then add the Chinese sausage, mushrooms, and onions. Fry this for a minute.

5. Now add the wine and continue to cook for 2 minutes.

6. Add the rice to the wok, and using a spoon, break it up so it is no longer in clumps.

7. Pour half of the sauce over the rice and mix well, continuing to break up the rice.

8. Mix in the rest of the sauce and continue to stir-fry until all the rice has been covered.

9. Mix in the scallions and add some white pepper.

10. Enjoy!

Nai Wong Bao or Cantonese Steamed Custard Buns

Pop these on a dim sum cart and they will be scooped up in a flash! These buns always bring back fond memories for me, and I hope you will enjoy making new memories when you make these for family and friends.

Time: 3 hours 15 minutes

Serving Size: 12 buns

Prep Time: 3 hours

Cook Time: 15 minutes

Ingredients for the Filling:

- 2 tbsp melted butter
- 3 tbsp heavy cream
- 3 tbsp all-purpose flour
- ¼ cup milk
- ¼ cup cornstarch
- ¼ dry milk powder
- ½ cup powdered sugar
- 2 eggs

Ingredients for the Dough:

- ¼ tsp salt
- 1 tsp yeast
- 3 tbsp powdered sugar
- 3 tbsp coconut milk
- 3 tbsp milk
- ¼ cup warm water
- 1 ½ cups all-purpose flour

Utensils:

- mixing bowls and spoon

- measuring cups and spoons
- medium to large pot which is big enough to accommodate the mixing bowl
- stand mixer
- kitchen towel
- parchment paper
- kitchen scale
- bamboo steamer
- rolling pin

Directions:

1. Begin by making the filling. Take your pot and fill it with about 2 inches of water.

2. When the water begins boiling, turn it down to a simmer.

3. Combine the eggs and sugar in a large heatproof or metal bowl and beat with your stand mixer on low.

4. Now pour in the milk and heavy cream, continuing to beat for a couple of seconds.

5. Sieve the flour, dried milk powder, and cornstarch and add them to the mixture. Continue to mix until the bumps disappear.

6. Combine the melted butter with the mixture.

7. Ask an adult to help you lower the bowl into the simmering water.

8. Quickly start to stir the mixture until it solidifies. It will look like a thick custard.

9. Remove it from the pan and let it cool down. When it has cooled, it will be ready to use.

10. While we make the dough, cover the custard to stop it from drying out.

11. Dissolve the yeast in the water.

12. You will let it sit for about 10–15 minutes, watching for bubbles to float to the top of the water. This is your sign to add flour, powdered sugar, salt, and coconut milk.

13. Using the dough hook attachment set on low, mix the dough and slowly add the regular milk 1 tablespoon at a time.

14. The dough should not stick to your hands or the bowl.

15. Cover the dough with a kitchen towel and leave it for an hour. We will now prepare the filling.

16. Divide the egg custard filling into 12 equal pieces and roll them into balls. To prevent them from drying out, cover them with a kitchen cloth.

17. You can now set up your steamer. We will start with cold water so there is no need to pre-boil the water.

18. Cut out 12 pieces of parchment paper; they should be 4x4 inches.

19. Check on your dough; it should be about 2 ½–3 times its original size.

20. Put the dough back in the mixer and mix for 2–3 minutes until all the air bubbles have disappeared.

21. Using your kitchen scale, divide the dough into 12 equal pieces. Cover them with a dry kitchen towel as you begin to work on assembling them.

22. Roll one of the balls into a 4-inch circle. The middle of the circle should be slightly thicker than the edges.

23. Place a ball of custard in the middle of the circle, pleat the top, and then close. Place it onto one of your parchment papers and put it in your steamer.

24. Repeat until you have assembled all the buns. Let the buns sit for 30 minutes before you begin to steam them.

25. Once 30 minutes have passed, turn on the stove and begin to steam the buns. You will only need to steam them for 12 minutes so set a timer.

26. Once 12 minutes are up, turn off the heat but leave the buns in the steamer and keep the lid on. Keep them in the steamer for 5 minutes.

27. The buns need this extra time to set. If you remove them too soon, they will collapse.

28. Once 5 minutes have passed, remove them and eat immediately. They are delicious as soon as they come out of the steamer!

Notes and Tips:

- Powdered sugar is also known as confectioners' sugar or icing sugar.

- The milk should be added 1 tablespoon at a time, and the amount may vary depending on the humidity in your area.

- If you do not have cornstarch, you can use wheat starch.

- You can replace coconut milk with regular milk.

- You can freeze any leftovers in a plastic bag and reheat them when needed.

Liu Sha Bao or Molten Custard Salted Egg Buns

A fun thing about food is that you get to use all your senses: taste, touch, smell, and sight. These buns will engage all of them as you pull apart the warm bun which oozes custard and take a big delicious bite.

You will notice that this recipe is very similar to the one above, but the difference is that this has a salty taste while the nai wong bao is sweet. I love the different taste options you can get with small ingredient changes like the ones we have made here.

Time: 2 hours 30 minutes

Serving Size: 11 servings

Prep Time: 2 hours

Cook Time: 30 minutes

Ingredients for the Dough:

- 1 tsp instant active yeast
- 1 tbsp baking powder
- 1 ½ tbsp water
- 13 tbsp milk
- ½ cup castor sugar
- 3 ¼ cups self-rising flour
- Ingredients for the Filling:
- 2 tbsp evaporated milk
- 3 tbsp custard powder
- 4 tbsp milk powder
- 7 tbsp unsalted butter
- ⅓ cup icing sugar
- 4 egg yolks

Utensils:

- mixing bowl and spoons
- measuring cups and spoons

- steamer

- potato masher

- baking paper

- clean kitchen cloth

- steamer

- sieve

Directions:

1. Let's begin with the filling by steaming your eggs for about 20 minutes. We want them to turn a bright orange. Using your potato masher or the side of a cleaver, crush the yolks until they become fine crumbs or a paste.

2. Incorporate the yolks, butter, evaporated milk, milk powder, icing sugar, custard powder, and butter together.

3. Firm up the mixture in the fridge for 20 minutes.

4. After 20 minutes, remove the mixture and form them into 1.2-inch wide balls. Place them back in the fridge as we move on to the dough.

5. Using your sieve, sift the flour into a bowl. Using your finger, make a hole in the middle of the flour.

6. Add the yeast, castor sugar, and baking powder into the hole and slowly pour the milk and water in.

7. Begin working on your dough incorporating the dry ingredients into the wet ingredients. Knead for 20 minutes.

8. Now add in the oil and continue to knead the dough until it looks smooth and waxy. This should take around 10 minutes. Pay attention to the consistency of your dough and add either flour or water depending on whether it is too dry or too wet.

9. Once you are happy with it, cover it with a kitchen towel and let it sit for 30 minutes.

10. Cut up 4x4-inch' squares from your baking paper.

11. During this time, the dough should rise and now you can knead it for an additional 2 minutes.

12. Section the dough into 11 portions and cover them in a towel.

13. Roll the ball until it forms a flat disk that is 0.2 inches thick and 4.7 inches wide.

14. Place some of the fillings in the middle of the flattened dough.

15. Using your hand, wrap the dough around the filling but leave a slight gap at the top.

16. Close the gap by sealing together the ruffled parts at the top of the bun. Twist the seal so that it closes tightly, trim off any excess dough, and then push it inward to flatten it. If you turn it upside down, it should be shaped like a ball.

17. Pop the buns onto your pieces of baking paper, making sure the seal is facing downward. Leave them for 1o minutes before steaming them.

18. Steam the buns for 10 minutes on medium heat.

19. Enjoy!

Mango Pancakes

A fruity and fresh sweet dim sum treat made with fresh mango, cream, and egg crepe—a perfect way to finish off your yum cha.

Time: 40 minutes

Serving Size: 8 servings

Prep Time: 10 minutes

Cook Time: 30 minutes

Ingredients for the Filling:

- 1 tsp vanilla extract

- 1 tbsp icing sugar
- 10 oz thickened cream
- 3 mangoes

Ingredients for the Crepe:

- 1 tsp vanilla extract
- 1 ½ tsp vegetable oil
- 1 ½ tsp unsalted butter
- ¼ cup cornstarch
- ¼ cup icing sugar
- 1 cup all-purpose flour
- 8.45 oz full-cream milk
- 4 eggs

Utensils:

- mixing bowl and spoon
- measuring cups and spoon
- 8-inch wide pan
- knife and cutting board
- whisk
- sieve

- cling wrap

- paper towel

Directions:

1. We will begin with the filling by cutting the mango into strips. Cut them about ½ inch thick by 4 inches long. Put them in the fridge or freezer until we assemble the crepes.

2. Put the thickened cream into a bowl and add 1 tablespoon of icing sugar and vanilla essence.

3. Using a whisk, whip up the mixture until it forms stiff peaks.

4. Place it in the fridge to cool.

5. Let's begin cooking the crepes by whisking our eggs.

6. Melt the butter and mix it with the whisked eggs, oil, milk, and vanilla extract.

7. Grab your sieve and sift the dry ingredients into the wet mixture. Fold in the mixture until it is well mixed together.

8. Now we will remove the lumps by pouring the mixture through the sieve.

9. Turn on the stove to low heat and add the oil. Use a piece of paper towel to spread it evenly across the pan.

10. Slowly and evenly pour about a cup of the batter into your pan. Move the pan in a circular motion to distribute the batter evenly so that it covers the base.

11. Continue to cook the batter until the top is no longer runny which should

take about 2–3 minutes.

12. Once the crepe is done, move it to a plate.

13. To keep the crepes moist while you cook the rest of them, cover them in plastic wrap.

14. Assembling the Crepes:

15. Let's put these together by first laying the pancake on a flat, clean surface.

16. Place some of the whipped cream in the middle of the crepe and put a mango piece on top of it.

17. Fold each side in so that it resembles a cushion or you could roll it like a spring roll.

18. Now pop it into the fridge for 15 minutes, with the seal-side down so that it can firm up.

19. Enjoy!

Tips and Notes:

- You can adjust the thickness of your crepes to your liking by using more or less batter.

Egg Tarts

Egg tarts are also called Hong Kong egg tarts or dan tat. They are small and round and are made of pastry that has been filled with sweetened custard.

This sweet treat can be found in Chinatowns and dim sum restaurants worldwide.

Time: 1 hour 40 minutes

Serving Size: 16 tarts

Prep Time: 1 hour 15 minutes

Cook Time: 25 minutes

Ingredients:

1. ⅛ tsp salt

2. 1 tsp vanilla extract

3. 2 tbsp cold water

4. 12 tbsp unsalted slightly softened butter

5. ½ cup evaporated milk at room temperature

6. ½ cup granulated sugar

7. 1 cup hot water

8. 2 cups all-purpose flour that has been fluffed and spooned into a measuring cup

9. 3 large eggs at room temperature

Utensils:

- mixing bowl and spoons
- mixing jug
- rolling pin
- whisk
- fine mesh strainer
- mini tart tins or muffin pan
- oven gloves

- toothpick

Directions:

1. Preheat the oven to 375 °F and place the cooking rack in the lower third of the oven.

2. We will be making the pastry first. Please make sure your butter is ready to work with. It should be soft enough that it is easy to break up with your fingers but not so soft that it collapses and forms a paste with the flour immediately.

3. Cut the butter into small blocks and add it to the dry ingredients above.

4. It's time to get messy! Work quickly and use your fingers to break up the mixture so that the butter, salt, and flour resemble coarse crumbs and there are small round balls of butter left.

5. Still using your hands, add the 2 tablespoons of water and bring the dough together. If you need to add a bit more water, do so, but only add ½ teaspoon at a time and not more than three. You want your dough to look quite dry and flaky.

6. Now we will let the dough absorb all the moisture and let it rest in the fridge. Wrap it up tightly in plastic and let it sit in the fridge for 20 minutes.

7. Put some flour on a flat surface where you can roll the dough, and once it has been rested, roll it out into a 6x15-inch rectangle. Work quickly as you do not want to overwork it which will make it dense and tough.

8. Take the top third of the dough and fold it down to the center, then take the bottom third and fold it over the top third.

9. It should be a smaller rectangle now and the seam of the folded dough

should be at the top.

10. Turn the dough once, either left or right, so that the fold is now on the side of the dough. Roll this out again into a 6x15-inch rectangle.

11. Repeat the folding steps above one more time.

12. Cover the dough and let it chill in the fridge for an hour.

13. Now we will make the filling.

14. Using a mixing bowl, mix your sugar into the hot water until it dissolves. Place it aside so it cools down to room temperature.

15. In a separate bowl, whisk your eggs, vanilla, and evaporated milk together then add your sugar water and continue to whisk that in as well.

16. By whisking so energetically, you have created bubbles that we want to get rid of.

17. Strain this mixture into a pouring jug using your fine mesh sieve to remove the bubbles. This is quite an important step as this ensures that the custard in our tarts is smooth and silky and looks glossy.

18. You should now have about 2–2 ½ cups of filling.

19. The dough should be ready to be worked with. Roll it out so that it is about 0.2 inches thick.

20. Cut the dough into circles that are about 4 inches big. They should be quite thin as they will expand as they bake.

21. Gently press your pastry dough into your muffin tray or tart tins. Be sure to leave a little bit of dough hanging over the tin so that it forms an

overhang.

22. Gather up any pieces of dough and roll them out so you can cut more circles. You should get about 16.

23. Fill the tart cups with your filling. This should be even.

24. Put the pan or your tins into the oven but immediately turn down the heat to 350 °F.

25. Bake the tarts for 26–29 minutes or until the filling has set. A good way to test this is to stick a toothpick into the middle, and if it stands up, it is done.

26. Now the hard part—allow the tarts to cool before enjoying them!

10
Teatime

Tea has been interwoven with Chinese culture for centuries and forms a very important part of our history and is even referred to as the national drink.

We have been drinking tea for thousands of years, and many believe the art of tea drinking began around 2737 B.C.E. (Parkinson, 2019a). At first, tea was considered a medicine as it helped with digestion, and people began to drink it after meals to help digest their food.

As time went on, tea making became an art form with special care given to the process of making tea. Tea became more popular and spread across China which eventually resulted in the creation of teahouses, places that were just for drinking tea.

There are four categories of tea:

- white tea
- green tea
- black or red tea
- oolong tea

White, green, black, and oolong tea come from the same plant, Camellia sinensis, but different varieties produce different teas.

The tradition of taking tea during dim sum is just as important as eating. Tea will be brought to you as soon as you sit down, and you will have a few options to choose from. Jasmine tea is usually the tea that is served when you sit down, but there are other teas you could choose from.

Since there are many different dim sum dishes, there are teas that are a better match for some of them than others. Below are six common types of tea that you will find served in a dim sum restaurant (Radez, 2015b).

Bo Lay or Black Tea

This tea has a strong flavor, and the flavor works well to counteract the oil in dishes that may be particularly oily. Black tea is considered to be the most traditional tea to serve with dim sum.

Guk Fa or Chrysanthemum Tea

This tea is light and refreshing. Unlike black tea which is considered a dark tea, chrysanthemum tea is considered refreshing and sweeter. These characteristics pair well with steamed dim sum dishes.

Guk Bo or Blended Black Tea and Chrysanthemum Tea

Your third option is to combine both teas. This offers you the best of both worlds.

Sau Mei Tea

This is a white tea that has an interesting taste that is both sweet and slightly bitter. It takes some getting used to, so maybe have a sip or two to try it out.

Luk Cha or Green Tea

This is a very well-known tea that is drunk for its refreshing flavor. You may be very familiar with green tea as it is served in most restaurants.

Red Tea

This is a strongly fermented tea and has a lovely sweet aftertaste. It originates from the Guangdong Province and is commonly found on the menus in local dim sum teahouses (Moychay.nl, n.d.).

11
Conclusion

Thank you for coming with me on this culinary journey through Cantonese culture.

I love how food can provide the tools to learn about the history, different ideas, traditions, and lives of other people across the world.

Not only does it teach you about others, but food and the practice of creating and sharing meals can make you learn many important life skills and lessons for yourself.

It is not all about eating, although that is one of the most fun and rewarding things about cooking!

Along with the joy that comes from eating a meal you have created yourself, I also hope that you feel a sense of pride in what you have managed to accomplish! You have learned a lot of new skills, and that is something to be celebrated.

I also hope that after you put down this book (and every time you pick it up again to cook), you do so with an eagerness to learn more about cooking not only because it is an essential skill but also because you have enjoyed the process.

Off you go and design your next dim sum menu for your friends and family!

We hope you enjoyed cooking and trying out the dim sum recipes in this book. If you did, we would be grateful if you could leave a review on your marketplace to help other kids discover the joys of dim sum cooking. Your feedback will help me continue to improve and create even more delicious and fun recipes in the future. Thank you for your support!

References

Asia Society. (n.d.). *What is dim sum? The beginner's guide to South China's traditional brunch meal.* https://asiasociety.org/reference/what-dim-sum-beginners-guide-south-chinas-traditional-brunch-meal#:~:text=Dim%20sum%20is%20a%20traditional

Asian Inspirations. (2019, October 28). *Asian tableware: The art of eating.* https://asianinspirations.com.au/experiences/asian-tableware-the-art-of-eating/

Aziz, M. (2020, May 17). *Cantonese style pan fried noodles.* Little Spice Jar. https://littlespicejar.com/cantonese-style-pan-fried-noodles/

Benton, J. M. (2017, April). *Learning about carbohydrates.* Nemours KidsHealth. https://kidshealth.org/en/kids/carb.html#:~:text=As%20with%20simple%20sugars%2C%20some

Britannica Kids. (2020). *Asian Americans.* Britannica Kids. https://kids.britannica.com/kids/article/Asian-Americans/352792

Britannica Kids. (n.d.). *Gold rush.* Britannica Kids. https://kids.britannica.com/kids/article/gold-rush/353191

Chen, M. (2021, August 26). *What is Cantonese food?* Rice Bowl Deluxe. https://ricebowldeluxe.com/what-is-cantonese-food/#:~:text=Cantonese%20food%20is%20a%20delicious

Chinese Food History. (2020). *Health benefits of Chinese food.* http://www.chinesefoodhistory.com/chinese-food-facts/health-benefits-of-chinese-food/

Eye on Asia. (n.d.). *Guangdong - A profile.* https://www.eyeonasia.gov.sg/china/know/china-municipalities-provinces/guangdong-profile/

Gallagher, S. (2021, August 5). *Top 10 reasons to teach kids how to cook.* The Spruce Eats. https://www.thespruceeats.com/reasons-to-teach-kids-to-cook-2098274

Guo, S. (2022, May 26). *Chinese tea house - Tea culture in China.* Chinatravel.com. https://www.chinatravel.com/culture/chinese-tea/tea-house\

Hair, J. (2007, March 13). *Chinese greens (yu choy) stir fry.* Steamy Kitchen. https://steamykitchen.com/43-chinese-greens-spinach-yu-choy-stir-fry-recipe.html

Joyful House Team. (2021, May 14). *3 Reasons why sharing plates is part of Chinese eating culture.* Joyful House. https://joyfulhouse.com.au/blog/3-reasons-why-sharing-plates-is-part-of-chinese-eating-culture/

Jumeirah. (n.d.). *10 things you need to know about Guangzhou.* https://www.jumeirah.com/en/article/stories/guangzhou/10-things-you-need-to-know-about-guangzhou

Keats. (n.d.). *Chinese tradition of eating together.* https://keatschinese.com/china-culture-resources/chinese-tradition-of-eating-together/

Kennedy, L. (2019, May 10). *Building the transcontinental railroad: How some 20,000 Chinese immigrants made it happen.* History. https://www.history.com/news/transcontinental-railroad-chinese-immigrants

KidsKonnect. (2017, September 22). *Symbolism examples, definition & worksheets*

REFERENCES 145

for kids. https://kidskonnect.com/language/symbolism/

Kidspot. (n.d.-a). *Chicken dumpling soup*. https://www.kidspot.com.au/kitchen/recipes/chicken-dumpling-soup/sr2wjn0p

Kidspot. (n.d.-b). *Chicken pot sticker dumplings.* https://www.kidspot.com.au/kitchen/recipes/chicken-pot-sticker-dumplings/q4tqrz1v

Kidspot. (n.d.-c). *Chicken wonton cups recipe.* https://www.kidspot.com.au/kitchen/recipes/chicken-wonton-cups-recipe/qkbixflw

Kidspot. (n.d.-d). *Wanton noodle soup*. https://www.kidspot.com.au/kitchen/recipes/wonton-noodle-soup/vzmu3ka5

Leung, B. (2020, October 5). *Sticky rice with Chinese sausage.* The Woks of Life. https://thewoksoflife.com/sticky-rice-with-chinese-sausage/#recipe

Leung, J. (2020a, August 17). *Zhaliang (fried dough rice noodle rolls)*. The Woks of Life. https://thewoksoflife.com/zhaliang-recipe/

Leung, J. (2020b, July 1). *Liu sha bao (Molten custard salted egg buns)*. Wok & Kin. https://www.wokandkin.com/liu-sha-bao/#recipe

Leung, J. (2020c, October 5). *Shumai: A Cantonese dim sum favorite.* The Woks of Life. https://thewoksoflife.com/shumai/

Leung, J. (2021a, January 10). *Cantonese steamed custard buns (nai wong bao)*. The Woks of Life. https://thewoksoflife.com/nai-wong-bao-custard-buns/#recipe

Leung, J. (2021b, January 23). *Steamed BBQ pork buns (char siu bao) recipe*. The Woks of Life. https://thewoksoflife.com/steamed-bbq-pork-buns-char-siu-bao/

Leung, J. (2022a, February 13). *Har Gow (dim sum shrimp dumplings)*. The Woks of Life. https://thewoksoflife.com/har-gow/

Leung, J. (2022b, January 20). *Youtiao recipe (Chinese fried dough)*. The Woks of

Life. https://thewoksoflife.com/youtiao-recipe/#recipe

Leung, J. (2022c, July 12). *How to steam food: 3 ways to set up a steamer*. The Woks of Life. https://thewoksoflife.com/how-to-steam-food/

Leung, J. (2022d, October 9). *8 Chinese Cuisines & how they differ*. The Woks of Life. https://thewoksoflife.com/8-chinese-cuisines/

Leung, K. (2022, January 7). *Taro cake (Chinese wu tao gou)*. The Woks of Life. https://thewoksoflife.com/taro-cake-wu-tao-gou/

Leung, S. (2021a, March 15). *Hong Kong egg tarts (Chinese dim sum/pastry)*. The Woks of Life. https://thewoksoflife.com/hong-kong-egg-tarts/#recipe

Leung, S. (2021b, September 12). *Chinese broccoli (gai lan) with oyster sauce recipe*. The Woks of Life. https://thewoksoflife.com/chinese-broccoli-with-oyster-sauce/#recipe

Livingston, L. (2020, October 24). *The ultimate guide to teaching kids to cook*. The Lean Green Bean. https://www.theleangreenbean.com/teaching-kids-to-cook

Marchetti, S. (2021, January 31). *The importance of sharing snacks, from dim sum to tapas*. South China Morning Post. https://www.scmp.com/lifestyle/food-drink/article/3119700/how-sharing-snacks-tapas-dim-sum-and-meze-feeds-primal-need-us

Millson, A. (2017, December 9). *Six rules for eating dim sum like a pro*. Mint. https://www.livemint.com/Sundayapp/8WTApbOKexojJe71XEWDVI/Six-rules-for-eating-dim-sum-like-a-pro.html

Moychay.nl. (n.d.). *Our red tea*. https://togo.moychay.nl/collections/our-red-teas

Oliver, J. (n.d.). *Barbecue chicken dim sum*. Jamie Oliver. https://www.jamieoliver.com/recipes/chicken-recipes/barbecued-chicken-dim-sum/

Parkinson, R. (2019). *Learn more about Chinese Cantonese cuisine and recipes*. The

Spruce Eats. https://www.thespruceeats.com/about-cantonese-cuisine-694173

Parkinson, R. (2019, June 26). *Ancient Chinese tea history and fascinating facts.* The Spruce Eats. https://www.thespruceeats.com/origins-of-chinese-tea-694325

Parkinson, R. (2022, April 25). *How to make Chinese steamed beef balls (ngao yuk).* The Spruce Eats. https://www.thespruceeats.com/steamed-beef-balls-recipe-694525

Pilot Guides. (n.d.). *Chinatowns of the world.* https://www.pilotguides.com/study-guides/chinatowns-of-the-world/

Radez, W. (2015b, February 25). *The best teas for dim sum.* Dim Sum Central. https://www.dimsumcentral.com/the-best-teas-for-dim-sum/

Radez, W. (2020, May 2). *7 essential kitchen tools for making dim sum.* Dim Sum Central. https://www.dimsumcentral.com/7-essential-kitchen-tools-for-making-dim-sum/

Rae, J. (2017, January 6). *Chinese spring rolls recipe with chicken.* Steamy Kitchen. https://steamykitchen.com/22276-chinese-spring-rolls-with-chicken-recipe.htm

Sarah. (2016, February 4). *10 of the best Chinatowns around the world.* Insight Guides. https://www.insightguides.com/inspire-me/blog/10-of-the-best-chinatowns-around-the-world

Ta, J. (2020, July 28). *Yum cha mango pancakes.* Wok & Kin. https://www.wokandkin.com/mango-pancakes/#recipel

Ta, J. (2021, February 24). *Steamed pork ribs with black bean sauce.* Wok & Kin. https://www.wokandkin.com/steamed-pork-spare-ribs-with-black-bean-sauce/#recipe

Tang, E. (2015, April 25). *Chive pancake.* Spice the Plate. https://www.spicetheplate.com/veggie/chive-pancake/

Wan, L. (2022, July 2). *Congee (Chinese rice porridge) recipe*. The Spruce Eats. https://www.thespruceeats.com/basic-congee-recipes-4065244

Weninchina. (n.d.). *Dim sum*. https://www.weninchina.com/dim-sum/

Worsley, G. (n.d.). *Pork and vegetable rice noodle rolls.* Kidspot. https://www.kidspot.com.au/kitchen/recipes/pork-vegetable-rice-noodle-rolls-recipe/dwteid3d

Yauatcha. (2019, August 16). *History of dim sum*. https://yauatcha.com/history-of-dim-sum

Zhuang, G. (2021, September 21). *The overseas Chinese: A long history*. UNESCO. https://en.unesco.org/courier/2021-4/overseas-chinese-long-history

Printed in Great Britain
by Amazon